Journey to

Joy

Journey to Joy

SARA CHAPPLE

Foreword By John Stickl

Photography by Debbie Slawter Photography

ISBN Paperback 978-1-7376717-1-8

ISBN Hardcover 978-1-7376717-2-5

Published by Purposed Publishing
www.purposedpublishing.com

"You are going to absolutely love Sara Chapple's book Journey to Joy! You will laugh, cry and most of all be filled with joy as you turn each page! I had a goofy grin on my face while reading her precisely thought-out words! I could not help but experience more joy in my life as I followed her journey to joy! It's practical, hope-filled and loaded with scriptures. No matter where you are on your joy journey this book will bless your socks off!"

Suzanne Manning, Mom of many & Co-author of Crazy Cool Family and co-founder of Crazy Cool Family Ministries

"Is happiness something that always seems just out of reach? Something you will have when you find the right guy, get your dream job, or go on vacation? Only when you get there, everything feels the same? My friend, Sara Chapple, would tell you that the struggle is real. In her new book, Journey to Joy, Sara shares her personal experiences on her way to finding true joy. With transparency and vulnerability, Sara will take you along on her journey. You will laugh, and you will cry, but most of all you will be inspired by what is possible in your own life. You will find that your Journey to Joy begins and ends, with your relationship with God. This book will be an amazing resource for you, but also one that can be used with your church small group, or over a cup of coffee with your girlfriends. One thing is for sure, you do not want to miss it!"

Barbie Armenta, Founder of The Brave Gathering and author of The Right Combination – Finding Love and Life after Divorce

"In Journey to Joy, Sara walks alongside her readers with wisdom, grace, vulnerability, and accountability. She reminds us that as life twists, turns, and detours, one thing remains consistent - God's presence. She invites us to flourish in the truths of God's love. She shares the keys to unlock the joy inside of us. Journey to Joy is fun, real, and inspiring. I am better because of it; you will be too."

Jacquetta Dantzler, Author of Find and Fulfill Purpose, Founder of Purposed Publishing and Purposed INC.

Dedication

This book is dedicated to all the joy-filled little girls.

If you know one, encourage her, celebrate her and share in her joy.

If you are one, dance, laugh, sing, and keep doing all the things
that bring you joy.

If you used to be one, my dear, she is still inside of you.
Your Father longs to take you on a journey to rediscover that
beautiful child and bring her into your present.

Epigraph

She was brave, fearless, funny, adventurous, trusting, and full of laughter.

She sang at the top of her lungs and did not care who heard.

She entertained her family with stories and performances.

She was kind and sensitive.

She was silly and goofy.

She made new friends.

She was empathetic.

She was confident.

She loved fiercely.

She played hard.

She danced.

She rested.

She loved.

She was full of light and joy.

           She was me.

           And somewhere along the way, I lost her.

This is the story of my journey to find her again.

           A journey with Jesus.

           A Journey to Joy.

Table of Contents

Table of Contents

Foreword

The human heart was created to live in joy. God designed us to live a life of receiving and releasing supernatural joy in every season of life. It's joy that fuels creativity. It's joy that enables us to dream. It's joy that builds life-giving relationships. It's joy that empowers us to live courageously. It's joy that enables us to walk through the chaos of this world while singing a song of hope in our hearts. We were made to experience the joy of God's goodness and grace. And that is why life is such a struggle when we lose our joy.

The Bible tells us that, "The joy of the Lord is your strength" (Nehemiah 8:10). If the joy of the Lord is our strength, then when we lose our joy, we will find ourselves weak. Defeated. Apathetic. Depressed. Unable to flourish in life. Unable to navigate the obstacles in front of us. Unwilling to engage with others. Unequipped to handle the challenges around us. Stuck.

Too often, we think the inverse of that verse is true. That it's strength that gives us joy. We tend to believe that once our circumstances are good (strong) then we will be happy (joy). But it's not strength that gives us joy, it's joy that gives us strength. It's the joy of the Lord, not the "joy" (happiness) of this world, that supernaturally strengthens us to live victoriously regardless of what is happening around us. Could it be that the reason so many of us live defeated lives is simply because we have lost our joy? Could it be that we have spent far too much time chasing personal happiness - a temporary feeling based on circumstances? Instead of journeying to joy - a lasting perspective based on what Jesus has done?

Romans 14:17 reminds us that, "The kingdom of heaven is righteousness, peace, and joy, in the Holy Spirit." This one verse gives us so much insight on the journey to joy. When I have been made right with God through Jesus, I will have peace in my heart. And when I have peace in my heart, I will experience joy in the midst of the circumstances of life. Righteousness leads to peace. Peace leads to joy. Therefore, the journey to joy starts with the finished work of Jesus. So, if you don't have joy, track it backward. If you have lost your joy, it's because you've lost your peace, and if you've lost your peace, it's because you've lost sight of the truth that in Jesus you have been made right with God. It's Jesus, and only Jesus, who can help us find true and lasting joy. He is the journey to joy. He is the King of the kingdom of joy. And no matter how long you've been gone he is always inviting you to come back home.

In *Journey to Joy*, Sara not only reminds us that it is time to come back home, she shows us the way. Like a skillful guide, she leads us down the path toward the joy that's available to us. Through personal experience, vulnerability, story-telling, and biblical insight she graciously points us toward a life of receiving and releasing supernatural joy. As one of the most joyful people I know, Sara has not only walked the *Journey to Joy*, she demonstrates it with her life. This book is the declaration of what she has been demonstrating for years – a life of supernatural joy! Her life inspires me, and I believe this book will inspire you.

So come on, what are you waiting for?
One.
Next Step.
At a time.
It's time to *Journey to Joy*.

John Stickl
Lead Pastor Valley Creek Church
Author of *Follow the Cloud*

Preface

What is Journey to Joy?

Well, it is a few things, really. It is a conversation with God I have been having for more than five years. Joy is something I felt was missing on a deep level for most of my adult life. Happy moments came and went on the surface, but few reached the deep places of my soul. It felt like there was a lid on my joy that was too heavy to lift. Ultimately, God showed me how it should look with a single picture - of me. From long ago. It all started there. She had a joy that I had lost and He told me we were going to get it back.

Since then, I have learned what genuine joy feels like. I have experienced freedom, peace, and joy and now I continue on that journey every day.

Along the way, I have discovered that my story is not unique. We all have moments and seasons where joy seems far away and unattainable. Many, like me, have lost a deep joy that they once experienced. Well, God says you can get it back. God says there is a kind of joy that is available every day, every season. I am still learning, still growing, and desperate to help others know this joy. To know there is light in the depths of depression. To know there is hope in a season of despair. And to know that on our happiest, most joy-filled day there is still more! More of God. More of His goodness and more of His joy available to us. And it is available right now.

Preface

I am not the guide; I am just a fellow traveler doing my best to follow the One who is our guide. I would love for you to join me. It is a journey with Jesus. A Journey to Joy.

To The Reader

The Journey to Joy is a journey through healing, freedom, identity and purpose. God wants to show us something in each of these areas. You will see the book is broken down into these four main sections along with *Preparing for the Journey* and our final section, *The Joy Journey.*

As you will learn, my journey to joy took place during a very difficult season with my dad. At the end of the Healing, Freedom, Identity and Purpose Sections you will see a chapter titled *"When the Road Gets Rough"*. These four chapters, spread out at the end of each section, will tell, in more detail, what the journey with my dad was like while I was on the journey to joy. You can read these one at a time as they are placed within the book, or you can choose to read those four chapters all at once. It is up to you.

How to embark on the journey – solo or with a group?

Journey to Joy can be read on your own or with a small group. Throughout the book you will find sections that are there just for you to reflect on and answer some questions about your own journey. These questions will allow you to walk out your very own Journey to Joy with God.

These are great group discussion questions as well. For groups, I recommend a six to eight week study depending on how much ground the group would like to cover in a week's time. Allowing one week for personal introductions and housekeeping, you could then have one week for each of the six sessions and then a closing week for a total of eight weeks, or finish in six by simply doing one week for each of the six sessions. Or create your own schedule that works best for your group!

I recommend using the *Journey to Joy Companion Journal* in your small group studies as it will better equip members to apply all they are learning, and you can share your official Mini Joy Journeys (explained in the journal) together!

As always, I'd love to know how you and your groups are doing on the journey! Snap a photo and use #JourneytoJoy so we can connect, and I can pray for you along the way!

Important Instructions Before You Proceed

I'd like you to officially give yourself permission to experience joy, in whatever form it comes. God means for you to. He created you to. I am officially giving you permission to as well. So, join us and give yourself the green light to experience all the goodness, all the fun and all the joy your Creator has for you!

Your permission slip:

I, _____Evica_____, hereby give myself complete access and full permission to experience the fullness of God's joy. To dance, to sing, to laugh out loud; to be exactly who God created me to be.

_____

Your Signature

INTRODUCTION

The journey to joy began as a conversation with God in my kitchen. I had recently gotten married to my husband, Paul, and become a new stepmom to three amazing kids. The five of us were taking a trip in a few weeks and my mind was already checking itself into the hotel.

I was imagining this upcoming vacation, but more specifically I was imagining myself on the vacation. This future vacation version of me was pretty similar to standing in my kitchen me. Except in one enormous way. Future vacation me had a joy about her that kitchen me could not seem to find.

Kitchen me was not miserable, don't get me wrong. Life was great. I was thirty-six when I finally got married that year, so I had waited and hoped and prayed for a husband and a family for a long time.

Now I had a wonderful husband and three amazing kids to boot! Plus, I got the three amazing kids with no stretch marks or morning sickness. Also, I don't pee when I sneeze. So, there's that. #stepmomsrule #allmomsrule

I was happy. But I felt like I could, and should, be happier. It felt like there was a lid on my happiness, a lid I knew was there but could not lift off. I was missing something. I had been missing it for a long time and I knew it. I had been to the lowest of low places in the past. And unfortunately, I would be there again before all was said and done. Seasons of depression had come and gone in my life. I did not feel the joy I was looking for during those times. When the seasons of depression would subside and I would feel better, I would of course expect to feel all the joy. You think, "I am no longer depressed, so I should feel all the good feels possible." But while I felt better when depression was no longer a part of my day-to-day, I did not feel joy. It just made me more aware of the missing piece. With the depression cleared away, it was even more obvious that there was a lid on my joy and happiness. I could feel happy and enjoy experiences, but it was as if I knew there was more joy and happiness I was capable of feeling, of expressing, I just did not quite know how to access it, so I was looking to the future to find it.

As I stood there imagining myself as future vacation me, I could see her and feel her so clearly. I could imagine myself being, feel myself actually being her. This version of me had a lightness about her. She was happy; only more than happy, she had joy. Genuine joy. She was carefree and not burdened by anything. She was having the time of her life, and I am pretty sure she wore a funny hat and danced a lot. I could not wait to be her. And it really felt like I would become her on this upcoming trip.

I do not know exactly when I thought the switch would take place. Maybe when we got to the hotel? As if there would be a package waiting for me at the front desk. I would walk up and say, "Anything for Sara Chapple?"

And the desk clerk would smile and say, "Why yes, Mrs. Chapple. In fact, this just arrived for you."

As he pulled a beautifully wrapped box from behind the counter, a spotlight from somewhere would make it glow a little and you would hear the faintest sound of angels singing. I would take the package to my room and carefully open it to reveal the most beautiful and, of course, perfectly fitting joy outfit. I would put on this "new me" outfit, spin around gleefully and announce, "TADA! Here I am full of JOY! Now let's have a perfect vacation!" Oh, and I would grab my hat. Because that is actual life.

As I came back to reality in my kitchen, I realized two disappointing things that day: The first was that I had done this little future me exercise before. Many times, in fact. I always seemed to

Introduction

look to some future time or scenario when I would finally be able to feel all the joy and happiness I felt like I should be experiencing. I would look to the future and imagine feeling a way I could never seem to make a reality in my present. The second realization was even harder to acknowledge.

Every time the trip or future event would arrive, I would not end up being her. I would still just be me, and the joy never came. I never actually got to transform into the joyous, future me I imagined. She only existed somewhere off in the distance. Much like me and Superman, you never actually saw the two of us together in the same place at the same time.

These two realizations made joy feel further away and more unattainable than ever before. Thankfully, before the despair could sink in, I sensed that still, small whisper of God with me in my kitchen.

What He said changed my life forever. He told me I had it all backward. Joy was not waiting for me somewhere far off in the future. I would not receive it on some upcoming vacation. I had already received it and I would take it *with* me

> All the joy that I felt I was missing was available to me right then.

on vacation. It was with me right then in my kitchen on a random Wednesday as I worked, cleaned the house, and made dinner. All the joy that I felt I was missing was available to me right then. Future me *was* kitchen me. Only better because kitchen me was real and here right now. I had all the joy, all the lightness, all the carefree-hat-wearing-dancing ability that I was imagining in future me.

God also explained to me why I could so easily picture this joy-filled version of myself. The reason I could see her and feel her was because I had been her before.

God gave me a picture in my mind that day. A picture of me as a little girl. He took me back to a point in my life when I had deep joy. I lived life to the fullest. I danced and sang; I was free.

3

Introduction

As I stood in my kitchen, I realized I could remember her. I could remember that time. It was a season when life was still simple and good. No divorces. No disfunction. No abuse. Life was good, but it was about to get hard. And this carefree, joy-filled girl was about to get lost. I was going to forget how to be her. I would still be able to imagine being her, I just would not be able to bring what I had lost into my present reality.

I lost some things I was not supposed to lose, and God wanted to show me how to get them back. They were still within me because He was within me, but they were buried so deep. If I would let Him, He'd take me on a journey to get it all back and learn how to experience joy again. That was the day my journey to joy began.

What I did not know that day was that we would be taking this "Journey to Joy" while I walked through the most difficult season of my life. Just one year before, doctors had diagnosed my dad with Parkinson's Disease. And while his health had been holding steady, it was about to be in steep decline. And I would step in as caregiver and have an up-close and personal seat as the disease ravaged his body and took everything from him. Ultimately, including his life.

It's funny how God works. Wouldn't it make so much more sense to teach me how to have joy when life is great and hitting on all cylinders? As always, God's ways are higher and better. (Isaiah 55:8-9) In times of difficulty, we are much more aware of our need for a Savior. We are more dependent, more open, and more desperate for a Word, an encounter, anything from Jesus. And so it was with my journey to joy.

The result was beautiful. Far from perfect, but beautiful in the way God can take our mess and brokenness and turn it into something majestic we never could have created on our own. My two-year journey with my dad was hard. More than hard. Whatever beyond hard is, that is definitely what it was. But it was also beautiful. I would not trade that time with my dad for anything. It was gut-wrenching, but it was a gift.

And for reasons I will never understand, God decided my journey with my dad, a journey in disease, and ultimately a journey through death would also be the timing of my journey to joy.

Your Journey

Journey to Joy is not just a story about my journey. As the author I think it's ok for me to say, "What would be the point in reading that book?"

No, the real point of this book is you and your journey to joy.

Do you want to get well?

The journey that God and I began that day in my kitchen is a journey He is inviting you on right now. It is a journey for all of us, no matter what the future holds. Make no mistake, it is a journey. Your feet might get a little tired on the way. The path may lead to some places long abandoned. But oh, sweet friend, the journey is a good one. And it is one you want to take with Him.

There is a story in The Bible where Jesus heals a man who had been crippled for thirty-eight years.[1] Jesus begins His interaction with the man by asking him a question: "Do you want to get well?" It is what He was asking me as we started on this journey to joy. I believe He is asking you that same question. Do you want to get well? Do you want to experience genuine joy?

The reason those two questions go together is that we have to do one in order to experience the other. The *Journey to Joy* is a journey of becoming well in the areas we are not. These areas are the things that hold us back from walking in all the joy meant for us.

---

1. John 5:1-17

Introduction

The journey I began that day with God took me down many paths. There was healing that needed to happen in deep places. There was forgiveness I had to process towards myself and others. We tackled the depression that had haunted me for so much of my life. He showed me areas of bondage in my life. Chains I had carried and lived with for far too long. Then He showed me how to be free.

He so sweetly reminded me of my identity in Him. I was His beloved daughter, but I had believed I was other things, other labels that this world had put on me. And finally, He showed me my purpose in this world and how to walk into all of that with Him. And as we journeyed, the joy began to grow.

Don't forget we did all of this while I walked through the toughest season in my life imaginable. He taught me how to experience joy again during what could have been my darkest time yet. Because He is God, and that is just how He rolls. He likes to show off and do the miraculous and the impossible - It's kind of His jam.

Will you invite Him to do the impossible in your life?

The same experiences are waiting for you. He wants to provide healing from your past, freedom in every area you are stuck. He wants to remind you that you are His beloved child. And oh, how He wants you to know that He created you on purpose for a purpose. He would love to walk that out with you. And all the while have you experience His great, inexhaustible joy.

The One who heals is asking you a question:

Do you want to get well?

PREPARING FOR THE JOURNEY

WHAT TO PACK?

If it hasn't become apparent yet, let me state it again, clearly: this is a journey. As the word itself implies, it is not an instant fix. God is a god of miracles, so I do not believe that if we begin this journey at forty, it is going to take another forty years to find the healing, freedom, identity, and purpose that bring genuine joy. But it also will not happen overnight. So somewhere in between. But seriously, God can do amazing things in amazingly short amounts of time, so do not let the fact that it is a journey discourage you. It is a journey worth taking!

I have some more good news. We do not have to wait to see an increase in our joy today. There are some specific things we can put into practice that will help us experience more God-given joy in our lives while we are going through this journey with Him.

Here are some quick tips to increase your joy today:

(The *Journey to Joy Companion Journal* can help you navigate through these Journey Essentials in more detail.)

Journey Essentials:

1. Regular time in the presence of God
2. Practice gratitude and thanksgiving
3. Worship

These three things alone will rapidly increase your joy. They are also powerfully connected.

> *"Enter His gates with thanksgiving and His courts with praise; give thanks to Him and praise His name."*[2]

> *"You make known to me the path of life; in Your presence, there is fullness of joy; at Your right hand are pleasures forevermore."*[3]

We see how these are all linked. When we practice thanksgiving and praise (worship) we enter into the presence of God and when we are in the presence of God, we experience the fullness of joy! That is what I like to call "Spiritual Math".

> Thanksgiving + praise = The Presence of God
> The Presence of God = Fullness of Joy

Making these three simple things a part of your daily routine will increase your joy. Not to mention your peace, hope and every other good thing God has for you.

We also cannot miss or ever forget the most important thing about real joy. It does not exist apart from God. In His presence is joy. The only reason we can experience joy is because of Him. We will find joy and experience joy in all sorts of ways, but only because it is first, and foremost, found in Him.

Joy can come in the *not* doing of something as much as the doing. Eliminating these next three things will exponentially increase your joy.

---

2. *Psalm 100:4*
3. *Psalm 16:11 ESV*

Things to leave behind:

1. Negativity
2. Complaining
3. Comparing

First, we'll look at negativity and complaining to make sure we are not bringing them with us.

"Do all things without grumbling or questioning"[4]

"Jesus answered and said to them, "Do not grumble among yourselves."[5]

"Do not grumble against one another, brothers, so that you may not be judged; behold, the Judge is standing at the door."[6]

"Let no corrupting talk come out of your mouths, but only such as is good for building up, as fits the occasion, that it may give grace to those who hear."[7]

The scriptures are clear. God is not a fan of grumbling or complaining. Can you blame Him? When we complain, we are being ungrateful. When my kids complain about dinner, they are ignoring what's been

> **When we let negative thinking run rampant in our minds, we are eliminating the possibility for joy to enter.**

given to them. They are being ungrateful. When we complain, the same is true. We are choosing not to be grateful for what God has done. When we choose to have a negative outlook, we are choosing

---

4. *Philippians 2:14*
5. *John 6:43*
6. *James 5:9*
7. *Ephesians 4:29*

to ignore the goodness of God in our lives. When we let negative thinking run rampant in our minds, we are eliminating the possibility for joy to enter.

Even on our worst day, there is still something that we can be grateful to God for. The fact that He exists is enough. Every single, tiny, good thing in our lives is from God. A roof over our heads and air in our lungs are two amazing gifts.

> *"Every good and perfect gift is from above, coming down from the Father of the heavenly lights, who does not change like shifting shadows."*[8]

Let's look at one last joy killer and make sure it is not hiding in our luggage somewhere.

Comparing

Theodore Roosevelt said, "Comparison is the thief of joy." I am not sure there is a non-biblical quote that I agree with more. When we compare our houses and our spouses, I guarantee we will lose our joy. When we compare ourselves to others or even to our old self, ("Oh, look how many wrinkles I did not have!"), we immediately cripple our joy.

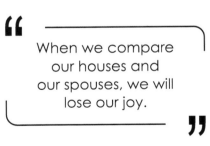

When we compare our houses and our spouses, we will lose our joy.

I do not believe that comparing is of God. There is always going to be a bigger, newer house (also car, wardrobe, furniture - you name it). That does not mean mine is no good! There is always going to be a husband who does something my husband does not do or one who

---

8. *James 1:17*

doesn't do something my husband does. Committing for better or for worse does not leave room for comparison. Also, my husband is not an object to size up. He is a person, made in the image of God, to love. When I compare myself to someone else, someone must come out as less than. So, either I or someone else created in God's image is deemed not as good. And this is the problem with comparison. It means we are looking for things that are wrong. We are looking for flaws. We are choosing to look through critical and critiquing eyes. We are not choosing to be grateful for what we have. In order to have a win in the comparison game, we have to now diminish another person and their life - there are no winners here.

When we compare, we invite the enemy to come in and do what he does best: steal, kill and destroy.[9] He steals our joy, kills our uniqueness and destroys our identity!

When we are tempted to compare, we can choose gratitude instead. When the thoughts of comparison start to flood your mind, stop and pray something like this:

"Lord, thank you for all the experiences these last years have brought me. Thanks for all the smiles and all the laughs that have left their mark (literally!) on my face. Each moment was a gift from you that I would not trade for the face of my twenty-year-old self. Really. Now, PLEASE Lord, help me keep this perspective for the next forty!"

Jesus gave some pretty sage advice to one disciple when he compared himself to another disciple. Peter asked Jesus about John and what John's future would hold right after Jesus told Peter that he would suffer and ultimately die for spreading the good news about Jesus.

Peter basically asked, "What about him, Jesus?"

---

9. John 10:10

I love Jesus' response:

> Jesus answered, *"If I want him to remain alive until I return, what is that to you? You must follow me."*[10]

"What is that to you?" It cracks me up every time. So anytime we find our minds drifting towards comparison to someone else, we should stop and realize it is none of our business what God is doing in their life. We should look for all the good He is doing in our own life.

Now that we have made some room in our bag by removing negativity, complaining and comparison, we have space for a few more items that will be beneficial on the journey.

More Journey Essentials:

* Get out into nature. Even if it is just your backyard. Preferably do this without technology. Being in creation will always draw you back to the Creator. And what do we find in His presence? (Hint: It rhymes with toy.)
* Do something for someone else. Regularly. Bake or cook for a neighbor. Ask your church about opportunities to serve or give back. Focusing on the needs of someone else gives us the opportunity to see all that we have and allows us to experience the joy of giving.

One last tip to prepare for the journey:

Pray and ask God to show you a time when you had genuine joy. Maybe He will give you an image like He did me. Or show you a memory. Find the picture, write out the memory or season of life.

---

10. John 21:21-22

Don't worry if nothing comes to mind right away. Ask, then listen in the coming days and weeks for God to speak. It may be in a dream or through a memory, but He will speak to you and answer you.

Looking through old photos can be a good starting point. Did something or someone ever burst your joy bubble? Pray and ask God to show you how you lost it. In the coming pages, I will equip you to process these areas even more with your Heavenly Father.

If genuine joy is not something you think you have ever experienced, talk to God about that as well. Ask Him to show you what it looks like in other ways. Maybe you will notice someone or something next time you are out running errands. Maybe you will begin to feel something deep inside, bubbling to the surface that brings a big smile to your face. Let it come! Ask God to see what His true joy looks like and prepare for Him to show you.

Trust the Lord to be your guide as we begin.

 Remember, we can increase our joy today by simply choosing to add and remove certain things from our life.

Joy Killers (Things we are leaving behind)

- o   Negativity
- o   Complaining
- o   Comparison

Joy Cultivators (Things we are taking with us)

- o   Time in the Presence of God
- o   Gratitude
- o   Worship
- o   Nature
- o   Serving others

15

WHAT IS JOY?

"And we all, who with unveiled faces contemplate the Lord's glory, are being transformed into his image with ever-increasing glory, which comes from the Lord, who is the Spirit."[11]

"You are the light of the world. A town built on a hill cannot be hidden. Neither do people light a lamp and put it under a bowl. Instead they put it on its stand, and it gives light to everyone in the house. In the same way, let your light shine before others, that they may see your good deeds and glorify your Father in heaven."[12]

While writing this book I have been blessed to have many conversations about joy with some incredible people. A common experience emerged in these conversations. In case this includes you, I would like to offer some freedom right now. There is a chance that someone, somewhere along the way made you feel embarrassed for your joy. Perhaps they shamed you or corrected you in some way that left you feeling like there was something wrong with you for expressing what you did, the way you did.

Can I just apologize on behalf of them right now?

I am so sorry they shut you down the way they did. I am sorry you felt like there was something wrong with you. Your joy and freedom made them uncomfortable because it exposed their lack of joy and freedom. They wanted to be as free and full of joy as you

---

11. 2 Corinthians 3:18
12. Matthew 5:14-16

16

were in that moment, but they could not so they tried to shut you down to make themselves feel better. I am so sorry.

I also want you to know your Heavenly Father saw you in that moment. More than that, He was with you. He was with you, and He felt your pain and your sadness. He loved you then and He loves you still.

Can you receive it? Will you begin the process of letting go and moving forward? God has great things in store for you in these pages. We start by letting go of the past to make room for all the good in the present.

> **We start by letting go of the past to make room for all the good in the present.**

When it comes to being shamed for our joy, we find ourselves in excellent company:

"And David danced before the Lord with all his might, wearing a priestly garment. So David and all the people of Israel brought up the Ark of the Lord with shouts of joy and the blowing of rams' horns."

"But as the Ark of the Lord entered the City of David, Michal, the daughter of Saul, looked down from her window. When she saw King David leaping and dancing before the Lord, she was filled with contempt for him."

"When David returned home to bless his own family, Michal, the daughter of Saul, came out to meet him. She said in disgust, "How distinguished the king of Israel looked today, shamelessly exposing himself to the servant girls like any vulgar person might do!"

David retorted to Michal, "I was dancing before the Lord, who chose me above your father and all his family! He appointed me as the leader of Israel, the people of the Lord, so I celebrate before the Lord. Yes, and I am willing to look even more foolish than this, even to be humiliated in my own eyes!"[13]

David's wife allowed David's expression of joy to make her uncomfortable. This was not David's fault. It did not reveal anything negative about David, but revealed everything about Michal. Deep down, I believe, she wanted to be as free as David. I believe she really yearned to express herself the same way David did. Instead, she tried to shame him. Thankfully, David was confident enough to not allow that shame to land on him. He was proud of his expression and defended it in the face of her scrutiny. But we will come back to David in a minute.

~~~~~~~~

I love words. I love them so much I even know the big nerdy word for people who love words - logophile. Even worse than that, I am an etymologist. This is an even bigger nerd word for people who study the origin and history of words. Not at all to be confused with an entomologist. Those crazy people study bugs.

So, when God first gave me an inkling that I was going to write this book, I did a deep dive into a word study on "joy". Specifically, I studied "joy" throughout the pages of Scripture. Do not worry, I will not take you through the same thorough analysis and force my love for all the words onto you.

Joy in the Old Testament

I have taken all the word nerd stuff and drilled it down to a few words that set the stage for us and the joy we are looking for. These first words are found in Zephaniah 3:17. This has become my absolute favorite verse in scripture, and I will gladly show you why.

---

13. 2 Samuel 6:14-16, 20-22

> *"The Lord your God is with you, the*
> *Mighty Warrior who saves.*
> *He will take great delight in you;*
> *in his love he will no longer rebuke you,*
> *but will rejoice over you with singing."*[14]

The first reason I love this passage is because God uses four original words to express joy. Four!

They are easier to see in a different translation:

> *"... He will <u>rejoice</u> over thee with <u>joy</u>; he will rest in his love, he will <u>joy</u> over thee with <u>singing</u>." (KJV)*

The first use is in "rejoice". Here we find the original Hebrew word: *"suws"*, which means "to be bright, that is cheerful, be glad, greatly, joy, make mirth, rejoice."

The second is "joy" and the original Hebrew word is *"simchah"* which means "blithesomeness or glee, exceedingly, gladness, joy (fulness), mirth, pleasure, rejoicing."

It's the third and fourth ones that really get me.

> *"... he will <u>joy</u> over thee with <u>singing</u>."*

Even though it's translated as "joy" again, the original Hebrew word was actually different. The word here is *"giyl"*, and it means "to spin around, usually rejoice, be glad, joyful, joy, rejoice."

> **"God will rejoice over you with dancing and singing." -saraphrase**

Before I can fully react, we have to see the last use of joy. Here it's translated as "singing". The original Hebrew word is *"rinnah"*

---

14. Zephaniah 3:17

meaning "creaking or shrill sound, that is, shout (of joy or grief) cry, gladness, joy, proclamation, rejoicing, shouting, sing, triumph."

Are you seeing this picture? Let me SaraPhrase it for you:

"God will rejoice over you with dancing and singing." -saraphrase

The Lord rejoices over us with singing and dancing! Can you let that sink in for a moment? The God who created the heavens, the vast solar system, every beautiful star in the sky, our world and everything in it – every gorgeous sunset and sunrise – the One who created you, has joy for you. And His joy causes Him to rejoice over you with singing and dancing. I pray that never loses its awe and wonder for me or for you.

Remember our buddy David who danced before the Lord with all his might? Do you see where he got his inspiration?

The word used to communicate David dancing before the Lord is yet another beautiful Hebrew word for joy or rejoice: "*sawchaq*", which means "to laugh, to play, to rejoice, including instrumental music, singing, dancing."

Our joy can be a physical and audible expression of all we are feeling, and I love to see these expressions of joy in people like David but more than anything, to see it in our Creator Himself.

Joy in the New Testament

My favorite thing about joy in the New Testament is its completeness. Right out of the gate we find joy and the cause for it:

"But the angel said to them, "Do not be afraid. I bring you good news that will cause great joy for all the people. Today in the

town of David a Savior has been born to you; he is the Messiah, the Lord."[15]

Jesus came. And He is the reason for our joy. He came for us. And the angles proclaimed that Jesus' arrival was a cause for great joy for ALL the people. That includes you and me.

I have always found it interesting that this is the moment His arrival is announced and that it would bring us great joy in *this* moment.

Why announce His arrival and all the joy as a little baby? Why not when He got baptized? Or was about to do some miraculous stuff? I imagine a big stage with lots of lights. And a hype man. Of course, Jesus would have the most amazing hype man. He kind of had a hype man, if you think about it.

The beginning of the good news about Jesus the Messiah, the Son of God, as it is written in Isaiah the prophet:

"I will send my messenger ahead of you,
who will prepare your way"—
"a voice of one calling in the wilderness,
'Prepare the way for the Lord,
make straight paths for him.'"
And so John the Baptist appeared in the wilderness, preaching a
baptism of repentance for the forgiveness of sins[16]

John the Baptist came before Jesus and made the way for Him. I guess that makes John the Baptist the first hype man. So, I picture John on the stage with a microphone to announce Jesus' arrival:

"Jesus is here!! Aaaaand He's about to heal some people! The blind are going to see! The crippled are going to walk, the lost

15. Luke 2:10-11
16. *Mark 1:1-4*

are going to be found, the dead are going to be brought back to life!!!! He's going to walk on water! And then He's going to turn water into wine! He's going to feed thousands and thousands of people with a couple of fish and loaves of bread! It's going to be amazing!!!! Without any further adieu... JESUS!!!!"

And the crowd goes wild.

But nope. None of that.

It is simply an announcement that He is here. A heavenly announcement, the best birth announcement that ever was. But He was just a baby. Why should Jesus as a baby be the cause of great joy for all the people? It's a baby. Yeah, it is Jesus, but it is *baby* Jesus.

Remember our Journey Essentials and what we find in the presence of God?

"In Your presence there is fullness of joy;"[17]

The fullness of joy is found in His presence, not in His miracles.

> "The fullness of joy is found in His presence, not in His miracles."

The joy that comes from God is available to us every moment of every day, because Jesus is available to us every moment of every day. The actual miracle is that He came, He is here now and He is with us every day. He is consistent and we can count on Him and He promises to never leave us or forsake us.

Before He changes anything in our life. Before He fixes anything. Can we just receive joy from the fact that He is in our lives?

What if nothing changed in your life? Ever. Things stayed just as they are today. What if you just had today and His presence? The

---

17. Psalm 16:11 (ESV)

Bible says that is enough to bring great joy to the people. Do you believe it is enough to bring joy to you?

One more question. Which people do you think had the most joy the day He arrived?

My guess is that it was Mary and Joseph. Then the wise men and shepherds. I think it was the people that were closest to Him that had the most joy in Him. Hmm. That is a connection that would be good for us to remember.

One last thing before we jump in. When Jesus rose from the grave and ultimately ascended to Heaven, He left us with a promise:

"And I will ask the Father, and he will give you another advocate to help you and be with you forever -- the Spirit of truth." [18]

The Spirit of truth is another name for the Holy Spirit and with the Holy Spirit came many amazing things. Our focus right now is on one in particular:

"But the fruit of the Spirit is... joy," [19]

Our advocate, the Holy Spirit, who will be with us forever, came and joy came with Him.

I know I promised not to overwhelm you with all the words but can I show you one more word for joy so you can see why I believe joy is available to us at all times? Even on our worst days.

The word used most often for joy in the New Testament, and the one that is in both Luke 2:10 and Galatians 5:22, is the Greek word *"chara"*. It is a "cheerfulness that is calm delight, gladness, exceeding joy".

Calm delight. On the day my father died, I did not dance before the Lord with all my might like we saw David do. My joy did not look or feel like that. I did not rejoice with singing and dancing. I am

Psalm 1 - our proximity to the Lord allows us to bear good fruit

---

18. John 14:16-17
19. Galatians 5:22

not saying it would have been wrong to do so. My dad was in heaven, he was no longer suffering and in pain. He could walk and run and do all the things his body did not allow him to do anymore here on earth. But I was not quite ready to rejoice that way on that day. But I can say I experienced the joy of the Lord.

I experienced this joy the New Testament has introduced to us. I experienced His calm delight. In the comfort of my family and friends and in the miracle of God's presence with me. My father passed away early in the morning on Sunday, March 10, 2019. He was living in an assisted living facility near my home and I was headed there to see him when I got the call that he was gone.

After talking to family and friends, I had one last phone call with my dad's dear friend, Lazette. None of those calls were easy, of course, and this one was no different. But as we wrapped up, she shared a very comforting story with me. Months earlier, while visiting my dad, they had a conversation about Lazette's mom who my dad had known well before she passed away. As they reminisced, they spoke about her mom's funeral. My dad shared he really loved a song that played at her service. It was a song called "Amazing Grace (My Chains Are Gone)" by Chris Tomlin. It was one of my dad's favorites and touched him at the service. After discussing it that day, they listened to it and enjoyed it together before Lazette left.

It was a touching story for her to share with me, and I was grateful for the memory of my dad. We wrapped up the call, looking forward to being together later in the week. With all the details taken care of for the day, it was time to head home. As my key turned in the ignition and the radio came to life, Chris Tomlin's voice suddenly filled my car with these words:

> *"My chains are gone, I've been set free*
> *My God, my Savior has ransomed me*
> *And like a flood His mercy reigns*
> *Unending love*
> *Amazing grace"*

As the song that Lazette and I had just discussed miraculously played on the radio station I just happened to be tuned to, I felt the presence of the Lord and a calm delight in knowing that my dad was with our Father in Heaven. The chains that were his wheelchair were gone; he had been set free. And like a flood he was fully experiencing all of God's mercy, love and amazing grace.

That joy, a calm delight, is for you. The joy that David experienced as he danced before the Lord? It is for you as well. The joy that our Father has for us is for all of us, it is for you. And it is for every moment of every day.

Can you believe and receive that truth for yourself? Have you ever seen a mustard seed? It is the tiniest little seed but see what Jesus says about believing with a faith that small:

> *Truly I tell you, if you have faith as small as a mustard seed, you can say to this mountain, 'Move from here to there,' and it will move. Nothing will be impossible for you.* "[20]

I just need you to believe a little bit. That is enough. God can and will take your mustard seed and together y'all will create the most joyfully beautiful, bountiful garden you could ever imagine.

We are on our way. Let's keep going.

Experiencing His healing touch is the next step on our journey.

---

20. Matthew 17:20

THE HEALING JOURNEY

THE JOURNEY BEGINS

"The Spirit of the Sovereign Lord is on me, because the Lord has anointed me to proclaim good news to the poor. He has sent me to bind up the brokenhearted,"[21]

"Hello. My name is Sara and I am an over-thinker."

"Hi Sara."

If there were such a thing as "Over-thinkers Anonymous" I would be a charter member. I probably could be the founder. I should probably start it. Why hasn't anyone started it? They probably tried and are still in a room somewhere thinking it all through and planning it all out. But we will never get to have a first meeting because we have to finish thinking through every possible scenario. Hmm, classic over thinkers.

Since I am an over-thinker, a simple question like, "Do you want to get well?", may never be allowed to be the simple question that it should be.

"Do you want to get well?"

Anyone in their right mind who is sick would say, "Yes!". Especially when the person asking actually has the power

> "Do you want to get well?"

to provide healing. Jesus was asking a paralyzed man in the Bible if

---

21. Isaiah 61:1

he wanted to get well. In my journey to joy, God was asking me the same question. He was showing me that the beginning of the journey to joy would be a journey of healing. A journey of going back to wounds that needed tending and a journey of giving and receiving forgiveness. He asked me if I wanted to get well. A normal person would just say "Yes!"

I, on the other hand, would say something more like, "Um, yes? Probably. Well, what all exactly is involved in this 'getting well' you speak of? Do I need a referral? What is my copay going to be?"

To be fair, getting well with Jesus, in the sense He was asking me, would not be the same as taking two aspirin and laying down for a nap. The healing Jesus wanted for me would not be an overnight fix. He would walk with me every step of the way, I would never do it alone, but I would need to be an active participant in my healing journey.

I am a visual person. I learn by seeing and doing. It was not completely surprising that early in this journey God gave me a picture in my mind of joy. An actual snapshot of me in a season of life when I was full of joy. I could definitely remember this time of my life. And I knew I had photos that represented the season He was showing me. Now, depending on how old you are, let me explain this concept to you.

Many, many years ago people, like me, used to take pictures with these big contraptions called cameras. No, not phones. Phones were attached to the wall and connected with long curly cords. Cameras were box like with a long lens. Just google it. They also had something inside of them called film. This film would magically capture the photos we took. But we could not see the images right away because the photos were tragically trapped in this roll of film until we took it to a developer. This person would then perform a series of scientific miracles to make the images appear on paper. Then, they would cut the paper into different sizes that we could purchase and bring home to put into glass frames or hang on the front of our refrigerators with magnets. I know it is crazy. I have many of these ancient relics, called photographs, in my home.

The Healing Journey

When God gave me this picture in my mind, I began digging to find an actual photo that represented the season He was showing me. And boy, did I find it.

When I came across the photos you see on the back cover, I cried. It was a mix of happy and sad tears. The images filled me with the joy that little girl carried with her. I could close my eyes and remember so much about her. Her lightness. Her carefree personality. She loved to sing and play and pretend. She loved to read and have adventures. She was the family entertainer, and she was a hoot!

One time she was performing, pretending to be a contestant, while the Miss America Pageant aired in the background. Then she slipped on her Fashion Plates because her mom's nightgown she was wearing as an evening gown was a foot too long. Her brother laughed at her, and she cried. But she got up and prepared for the all-important interview round. I remembered being her. With those pictures, God helped me remember what that genuine joy felt like.

But there were also tears realizing how far I had drifted from being her. In the sweet way that only He could, God told me again how I had lost some things I was not supposed to lose, including my joy, and He wanted to help me get it back. He wanted to take me on a journey and show me how to get back the things I lost that I was not supposed to lose.

The little girl in that picture was well. Most of us are at or around that age. It is before life really throws anything at us. But, unfortunately, for that six-year-old little girl, life was winding up and about to start throwing.

I have to add a bit of an editorial comment before this next section. I have wrestled and struggled with this part for a while. Telling my story is very easy for me. But when the troublesome parts of my story become intertwined with other actual people and their stories, it gets complicated. In books, authors often change the names to protect the innocent. I cannot really do that because parents are parents and certain players cannot be hidden or protected because they just are who they are. God blessed me with two amazing parents. I love them and I am so glad they are mine. They were present in my life, and they loved me. They taught me so much and I have a lot to be grateful for and I am. Of course, they were not perfect. No parent is. No human is. None of our grandparents were perfect, either. I know, that is a hard one. Grandparents are THE definition of perfect humans. But while they may have been perfect grandparents, they most definitely were not perfect parents. There are no perfect parents. All my kids will be able to write books about how imperfect I am. That is not what I am trying to do here. The point is not to show the mistakes that anyone made. Except mine, I guess. I made plenty and I'll be happy to elaborate and expound on those for your learning enjoyment. But forgive me if I do not dwell on or detail the imperfections of others. Especially the others that I love so much and am grateful to have had in my life.

So, back to the life throwing at me season. I think the easiest way through is simply sharing the facts:

When I was about six years old, my parents divorced. In that season, the entire picture I had of my family actually got turned upside down. I learned I had two half-brothers I had not known about previously and *my* brother, his name is Clint, that I knew and loved and looked up to like crazy, was technically my half-brother as well. Thankfully, that never impacted our relationship, and we always were and are very close to this day.

As an adult, I realize the value of family in every shape and size, and I love all the additions that have come! But for that little girl it was a scary, confusing and unsettling time.

Because of some remarriages, I also had some step-brothers during that season. One, at the age of fifteen, thought it would be cool to be inappropriate with his new little step-sister. I was only eight. Thankfully, that marriage and living arrangement did not last long. The events that occurred in that situation came back in bits and pieces when I was eighteen-years-old. Before then I did not even remember that my step-brother existed because I had suppressed the memories so deep. Great Christian counseling helped me recover and remember enough to heal, forgive and move forward, but at the time the damage was definitely done.

Before 4th grade, my mom and I moved from Lubbock, Texas to Dallas, Texas. My dad and Clint stayed behind. Clint is nine years older than me, so he was transitioning into college. My mom's parents both passed away over the next couple of years and we moved again and I changed schools one more time after 5th grade. For whatever reason, in my new school in 6th grade I did not find my place or my people. I found a group I wanted to be friends with, that it felt natural to be friends with, but after a few months they voted me out of the group. Yes, voted me out. Being a kid can be rough. I had always made friends easily, but this time it just did not happen. I felt like an outcast, and everything from the previous few years seemed to catch up to me. I guess it was the straw that broke me. I know all the years leading up to that one were hard, but this was the first time I remember it actually *feeling* hard. The first time I remember tears and sadness. The first time I felt lost and broken.

Can I share a cool redemption story with you though?

I went to school with almost all of those girls until we graduated from high school. Of course, they all were, and are, incredible and amazing people. And we all did end up being friends as we matured and grew up.

My senior year I was hanging out with one of them and we were just talking and for some reason she brought up the whole "voting out" debacle of 1990. Don't do the math. It was a minute ago.

Anyway, she apologized. She said she could not imagine how tough that must have been for me to go through. Of course, all was already forgiven but it meant so much for her to say it.

In the 6th grade, I embraced the "having stuff thrown at me" experiences so much that I picked up the ball and started throwing it at myself. I started rebelling. My first act of rebellion was stealing cigarettes from my mom.

I still remember stealing that first cigarette. My mom left her purse out and a pack was right near the top. She was not in the vicinity, although our house was not that big. I must have been feeling very brave or in need of some sort of adrenaline rush that day. I took a chance, grabbed the pack and as quickly and ninja-like as I could slid one of those Marlboro lights right out of there like I had a pack a day habit. For the record, she successfully kicked that habit a long time ago and is no longer a smoker. Not that I am judging, as you will see, I have no room to throw stones.

I waited until the next time I was home alone and with my heart racing, I ran out to our backyard and smoked my first cigarette. I did not know what I was doing, but I guess I decided I liked it because it was the first of many that I stole and smoked for a while.

It was also at this time that I realized life felt a tiny bit out of control. Just a smidge. Unfortunately, like many girls around that age, I developed an eating disorder. Fun times. I also realized that certain attention from certain people (see also: boys) made me feel fantastic. It seemed to fill up a hole inside of me a bit. Thankfully, stealing and my life of crime never really took off. But the rebellion certainly did. So did the eating disorder and craving attention from the male species. It is easy to see the areas forming where I would need the healing touch of Jesus.

Fast forward to me at twenty-four-years-old. It is probably a story that many people identify with, even if just a little. I had been lied to, abused, taken advantage of, made fun of, overlooked, pushed aside. I experienced death, divorce, disappointment, and addiction. I made choices I thought I never would and wished I never had. I was tired, alone and afraid. I did not recognize the person I had become. In my desperation and brokenness, I did the only thing I could think of, I cried out to God.

It was then that I decided to make God and His church important priorities in my life.

> I did the only thing I could think of, I cried out to God.

MEETING THE HEALER

When I was very young, and my parents were married, we all went to church. My dad told me about a conversation we had when I was five-years-old. He told me that he grew up thinking that the only way for a person to accept Jesus was to be in a church service where they did an altar call and you go down front and pray and ask God into your life. He wanted to make sure I knew I could do that anywhere, at any time. He said my response was "Oh daddy, I already did that."

I believe him, I just don't remember. I can look back on certain moments growing up where I felt like God was definitely with me. Guiding me and leading me. I certainly did not always listen, but I can see where He was with me, drawing me to Himself.

As a teenager and young adult, I did not really understand what being in a relationship with God meant or looked like. I believed in God, but there was not any evidence in my life to support the fact that I believed.

At twenty-four, when I felt so broken and alone, the only thing I could think to do was go to church. I somehow knew enough to know what I needed was God. But God in a way I had not known Him before.

In that season, God went from being some figure up in the heavens to a real, up-close and personal presence in my life every day. And because of

> **I needed God in a way I had not known Him before.**

that, I started to change. My life began to look different. Healing was taking place.

By the time God and I were having the conversation about joy in my kitchen, I had been walking with Him for about ten years. Quite a bit of healing had already taken place over that time. Realizing I was already part of the way through the healing journey was encouraging. A lot of prayer and time with God and professional counseling helped me process much of my childhood. I would say the major theme of that healing journey was about acknowledgement and forgiveness.

I first had to look back at all the things that happened. Things that happened to me and things I had chosen on my own. It was not about looking back for the sake of looking back. It was about letting God into all those places. Walking back with Him. Letting Him show me He was still with me, even in the hardest moments. He never left me or abandoned me. In many cases, I could see where He protected me from it being so much worse.

Once I was willing to go back there with Him, I had to look and see where forgiveness was needed. I had lots of opportunities to make sure I had forgiven others and had released them and what they had done. God did not want me to carry around any offense or bitterness. For me, at least, this was not a one-time process. As I began my journey, God showed me areas where I still needed healing. I would forgive someone and find that lightness I knew came with real forgiveness, and then over time I would eventually realize some part of the offense had crept back in. I would need to forgive again. Say it again and tell God, "I forgive them." In every case, the forgiveness eventually took and I could move forward free and clear.

It did not happen overnight. The process took time. I knew I was there when I could pray for the person who hurt me. Really pray for them and mean it. Pray for God to bless them and their relationships.

Another indicator for me was how I spoke about these people to others. Could I speak well of them or only speak of them as a villain who had wronged me? Did I want to tell the story of how I was hurt to gain sympathy? These were all indicators that I had not truly forgiven that person. My pastor puts all of this into three simple (not necessarily easy) steps.

Step one, I focus on God's grace for me. I have been forgiven for so much! God has never withheld His forgiveness from me. When I remind myself of all He has forgiven me for, it helps me realize I am in no position to withhold forgiveness to someone else.

The second step is one I have already mentioned, pray for them. This may even be what moves us along the forgiveness pathway. Maybe when we first utter the words, we do not fully mean them yet. It is ok. Say them anyway and pray for God to get you to a place where you can mean it.

The last step is my favorite even though it is the hardest, but for me it is a clear indicator that I have forgiven, and I am free from all bitterness and resentment; bless them. He also calls this crediting their account. Can I do something to bless them? Maybe they know about it, maybe they do not. It is not necessary that they know. This process is for our healing journey. Perhaps we begin blessing them by not speaking negatively about them ever again. We bless their reputation by not smearing it all over town and instead we speak well of them. We can bless them in tangible ways as well. My encouragement is for us to be willing to bless them in any way that God invites us to.

When we can take these steps, we will truly have forgiven anyone who has hurt us.

THE TIME TO FORGIVE

One thing God showed me right away on the healing journey was that the time to forgive is now. Right now. Every second I choose not to forgive is a second too long. It is a second I am choosing to give away to the enemy. Only I hold the power to stop it. My forgiveness will release me from it all in a way I may have never thought possible. It does not take time to forgive. Not according to Jesus.

In the Gospels we find the account of the crucifixion of Jesus. In Luke Chapter 23 Jesus had been arrested, accused of crimes He did not commit, beaten, spat on and finally nailed to the cross. It is after all this happened and the crucifixion is in the process of happening that Jesus says these words:

> **"** *the time to forgive is now* **"**

"Father, forgive them for they know not what they are doing."[22]

Jesus forgave the very people who were killing him while they were killing him!

I know what you are thinking, "Sure, Sara, but that was Jesus. He was perfect. No regular human could ever actually do that."

---

22. Luke 23:34

I am so glad you said that because I have two very good arguments.

The first is in the book of Acts, where we find a man by the name of Stephen. The Bible says that he was "a man full of God's grace and power"[23]

Stephen served faithfully with the other believers after Jesus ascended to heaven. Unfortunately, the hate that led to the crucifixion of Jesus was still alive and well. Stephen was ultimately falsely accused as well and stoned to death. It is in his last moments, as he is being stoned to death, where he says:

"Lord, do not hold their sin against them."[24]

Stephen, a regular man, prayed for God to forgive his attackers while he was being attacked. He modeled Jesus' example, and I believe that means we are capable as well.

My second argument is that the very power that flowed through Stephen in order for him to be able to forgive his own murderers, also empowers you and me. Remember your objection, "No regular human could ever do that."

I believe that statement to be true, no regular human could ever do that. The lie is in believing that you and I are regular humans.

Remember, Stephen was a man "full of God's grace and power".

In 1 Corinthians chapter 3, the apostle Paul is encouraging the Corinthians to live godly lives amid the world they were living in. In the course of doing this he asks them, "Are you not acting like mere humans?"

Paul's belief is apparent. They were not mere humans, so why were they acting that way?

You, Stephen, and I are no mere humans. When we trust Jesus, we are full of God's grace and power. We are capable of so much more than a mere human. Because of God living in us, it is possible

---

23. Acts 6:8
24. Acts 7:60

for us to do the seemingly impossible, even forgiving our offenders while they are still hurting us.

I am not saying that this is easy. It is not. It is not easy or trivial or inconsequential. Just the opposite. This is so important for you and me in our journeys to find healing and joy. We cannot and will not experience all the joy God has for us if we are not willing to lay our offenses at the feet of Jesus and forgive those who hurt us.

> **When we trust Jesus, we are capable of so much more than a mere human.**

The repeated verbal and emotional abuse I experienced in a season my life from one individual was not at all easy to forgive and lay down. For years I even proudly wore the banner of victim, wanting to tell my story to all who would listen. I believed I had a story to tell, and I thought that was it. Until God came into my life and showed me, that was not my story at all. I was not a victim; I was a victor in Him because of Jesus. I am not here to say one day I just forgave, and it was done just like that. But I made up my mind that one way or another I was going to forgive them. Walking it out took time, but I knew that was what I wanted. And by God's grace, He got me there.

I also had to go through the same forgiveness process with myself. I made some awful choices in my teens and twenties. I had a lot of pain inside and tried every worldly way I could find to fill it. Food, drugs, alcohol, tobacco, relationships with men, striving, perfectionism...the list goes on. I had to be willing to look at all of that with the Lord. Own it, then release it to Him and receive His forgiveness, forgive myself and then MOVE. ON.

Anytime the enemy wanted to bring up my past to slow me down or discredit me, I had to remind myself of the forgiveness and the release that had taken place. I had to choose not to let the enemy distract me or keep me in my past. I could not embrace all God had for me in the present if I was stuck in past offenses or guilt and shame. I had to choose to believe Romans 8:1:

"Therefore, there is now no condemnation for those who are in Christ Jesus."

My other choice, as someone who spoke and taught the Word of God, was to share it. I brought it all out into the open. The enemy's power is diminished when we bring into the light that which he has tried to shame us with in the dark. As I began teaching and sharing in my job at my church, I talked often about my past and the things I had done and how far God had brought me in my journey. I found so much healing this way. I could connect with others who identified with different parts of my story and realizing I was not alone in my past struggles gave me strength to keep sharing and keep allowing God to bring it all into the light.

The healing journey is a process of bringing any area of our lives where we are "unwell" to God. For me that involved a lot of forgiveness and letting go and then it involved letting Him into the scary places of my life where I had been battling, and losing, on my own.

Releasing these areas fully to God moved me forward in my journey as a more healed and whole person. Being healthy is a huge part of being able to walk in the fullness of all the joy He has for me! And the same is true for you.

YOUR HEALING JOURNEY

For all of us, the healing journey begins with knowing the places where we are not well. We have to look back at those places with God to see where unforgiveness, bitterness, or resentment, might be lurking. We must invite God to shine His light on anything that is keeping us stuck and stealing our joy.

> *"Search me, God, and know my heart; test me and know my anxious thoughts. See if there is any offensive way in me, and lead me in the way everlasting."*[25]

We all have a past. We have all been hurt. The stories vary, but the results are the same. We have been wounded. But our God is the Healer. And He never meant for us to be the walking wounded. He means for us to be well. We can trust Him with all the hurts of our past because He is a good God. What He wants to take from us is for our good. Sometimes we hang on to things simply because we find comfort in the familiar. We have carried this hurt, this offense for so long we do not even know what it would be like to lay it down. Can you trust Him enough to try?

Remember the man that Jesus healed from earlier in the book? He had been crippled for thirty-eight years! Nearly forty years of carrying his hurt, his pain. In one instant Jesus takes it from him, but the man had to be willing. The man picked up his mat and walked!

---

25. Psalm 139:23-24

He had to make the choice to get up and leave his life of being crippled in the past.

God means for you to be well. Holding on to the hurts of your past will always keep you from walking in the full joy He has for you in the present.

> Holding on to the hurts of your past will always keep you from walking in the full joy He has for you in the present.

1. As you look back at your life, what were the big hurts and traumas that you experienced? Remember, we are not trying to live in the past. We look back to identify areas where we are stuck and unhealthy. Then, we take these areas immediately to the Healer so we can move forward healed and whole.

_____

_____

_____

_____

_____

_____

_____

_____

_____

_____

2. Do you sense any areas where you are hanging on to unforgiveness toward others? Yourself? Maybe you have forgiven in the past, but a sense of bitterness or unforgiveness has crept back in. Forgive again. Give it over to God again. Tell him out loud that you forgive. Write it down. Ask Him to help you forgive if you feel stuck on the words. He will help you get to that place.

_____

_____

_____

_____

_____

_____

_____

_____

_____

_____

3. Ask God to help you move through the three areas of forgiveness my pastor teaches:

   I. Receive God's grace and forgiveness for yourself.
  II. Pray for those who have hurt you.
 III. Ask God to show you how you can bless them and "credit their account."

_____

_____

_____

_____

_____

_____

_____

_____

_____

_____

4. Part of my journey involved bringing things out of the dark and into the light by sharing them. Do you have a trusted, godly relationship or a Christian counselor where you can bring things in your past into the light? I encourage you to pray for these relationships if they do not already exist. Jot down some names or write out a prayer to God asking Him to bring these people into your life.

_____

_____

_____

_____

_____

_____

_____

_____

_____

Remember, forgiveness does not mean that what happened is okay. It simply means that we trust God to carry the burden of it, not us. We hand it over to Him. It is okay that we tell Him how we feel. If you are struggling with the words to say, try this:

"God, this was not okay. I am angry and sad and hurt that this happened to me. I do not understand. But I do not want to continue to be hurt by it because I choose not to let it go. I want to be free and healed, so I release it and them to you. I forgive them and I trust You to help me mean it and walk forward in this forgiveness."

I believe eventually God can get us to a place of being able to pray for those who have hurt us. That might seem totally crazy to you in this moment, but I can tell you from experience that it is very possible, and it is so healing. Ask God to help you get there and you will in Jesus' name.

WHEN THE ROAD GETS ROUGH I: *A Fight For Joy*

S ometimes in life the Journey to Joy becomes a fight for joy.
One of, if not the most ironic things about my joy journey was how it all culminated in a season of great trial and suffering. Side note: I wonder if Jesus' greatest joy came at the time of His greatest trial and suffering?

As I have stated previously, the timing for my journey to joy ended up coinciding with my dad's final journey on this earth. As his primary caretaker, I had a front-row seat as he fought bravely in a battle against Parkinson's. In case you were wondering, this would NOT have been the timing I would have chosen to be learning all about joy. This would have been somewhere near the bottom of that list. I can't think of much else that would have been below it.

The trials and obstacles that we face threaten to steal the joy we have worked hard for. When those times come, we must be diligent and willing to fight for what is still rightfully ours. God's promises are not contingent on our circumstances being perfect. In fact, scripture tells us plainly:

"for God's gifts and his call are irrevocable."[26]

The full life He promises us in John 10:10 is not conditional. We can have that life in Him, every day. Even the hard days.

---

26. Romans 11:29

When those days or seasons come, it is so important for us to, first, acknowledge that we are in fact in a fight. We have an enemy. He does not want us to experience the joy of the Lord. Ever.

Ephesians 6 tells us plainly we are in a battle. We must first understand that.

> *"Put on the full armor of God, so that you can take your stand against the devil's schemes. For our struggle is not against flesh and blood, but against the rulers, against the authorities, against the powers of this dark world and against the spiritual forces of evil in the heavenly realms."*[27]

But Ephesians 6 does not leave us high and dry in this battle. We are in a fight but:

a.   We have weapons to fight with!

> *Therefore, put on the full armor of God, so that when the day of evil comes, you may be able to stand your ground, and after you have done everything, to stand. Stand firm then, with the belt of truth buckled around your waist, with the breastplate of righteousness in place, and with your feet fitted with the readiness that comes from the gospel of peace. In addition to all this, take up the shield of faith, with which you can extinguish all the flaming arrows of the evil one. Take the helmet of salvation and the sword of the Spirit, which is the word of God.*[28]

And

b.   The Bible makes it clear, we never fight alone!

> *But the Lord stands beside me like a great warrior.*

---

27. Ephesians 6:11-12
28. Ephesians 6:13-17

Before him my persecutors will stumble.
They cannot defeat me.
They will fail and be thoroughly humiliated.
Their dishonor will never be forgotten.[29]

"For the LORD your God is the one who goes with you to fight
for you against your enemies to give you victory."[30]

When the unexpected comes, we need to remember that it was not unexpected to God. We may not know the answer, but we know the One who does.

We can choose to have His perspective on our situation. We can take a step back with Him and see a bigger picture. As we just saw, we can trust Him to fight our battles for us.

We can trust Him to heal our hurts and be near to us in our broken heartedness.[31]

We can lean on the body He has placed us in to comfort us and help us in our time of need.[32]

We can remind ourselves that our Father in heaven rejoices over us with singing and dancing. He takes delight in us each and every day.[33]

And the best reminder of all:

"I can do all things through Christ who strengthens me."[34]

Thankfully, because of God's amazing timing and goodness, I could do all of this and more while I walked this road with my dad. Somehow, through it all, my joy grew. It never left me and helped me through when I could not find another way. It was a journey to joy,

---

29. Jeremiah 20:11
30. Deuteronomy 20:4
31. Psalm 34:18
32. Galatians 6:2
33. Zephaniah 3:17
34. Philippians 4:13

but in these instances, it was most definitely a fight. A fight that I won because of all I'd learned on my journey.

Where are my planners at? Oh, how I love to plan. This book had a plan. A very nice, succinct one. But some things happened I did not plan for that almost kept this book from becoming a reality. When God and I first started talking about joy, my dad had recently been diagnosed with Parkinson's Disease. He was only a few months in, and he was not very sick or showing many symptoms at all.

Over the course of this journey, he did get sick, and the symptoms got worse and worse. Then, while writing a Journey to Joy, my dad passed away.

In case you haven't kept up: A girl who struggled most of her life and who had trouble finding joy and who now has a father who is dying - let's have her write a book about joy.

Why? Who on earth would ask that person to write a book about joy?

Girl, I have asked God that question so many times. I guess the answer is, nobody on earth would do it. But someone in Heaven would.

The truth is the journey to joy in my life has been a very intentional one. And at times it has very much been a fight for joy and a fight to keep that joy. I must remind myself that joy is a part of the package deal I got when I became a daughter of the King. It is my right. It is available to me. The enemy will try to steal it, but I do not have to let him. The joy from the Lord is mine to enjoy and walk in.

There may be some who awake 365 days a year full of joy, overflowing, and that is so awesome. I love that!

That just has not been my journey. That same joy is available to me 365, but for various reasons it has felt hidden, at times I have not chosen it. And at times depression and gut-wrenching circumstances have made it seem impossible to find. Emphasis on "seem", because I believe whole-heartedly joy is always there. Always in me and always in you. We just have to learn the truth and then decide to believe it day after day after day.

The Healing Journey

In the midst of my journeys: the healing, freedom, identity and purpose journeys, I was on another journey as well. I was on a journey with my dad. It turned out to be his last journey. And thankfully, I got to be with him every step of the way.

Things can feel out of control when our health is not great. But when it's the health of a loved one, it feels even more out of our control. While I wrote this book, I watched my dad die. Day after day, week after week.

But through the miracle that is God, we had joy in the middle of it all. We had laughter. We had jokes. Oh, we always had jokes. Even when we probably should not have. We had jokes. Joy in the tough times might seem crazy. I get it. But it is not for those of us who follow Christ.

For the message of the cross is foolishness to those who are perishing, but to us who are being saved it is the power of God.[35]

Yep. It will seem crazy and impossible to some. But that does not mean it is not true, and it does not mean I cannot live it out in my life.

Having joy during difficulty also does not mean we do not care. I think it means we do care. It means we care enough to stay in the game. To not get counted out or benched because of our despair. I would not have been much help to my dad in that season if I was full of hopelessness. That was not what he needed.

It is not about wearing a t-shirt every day that says, "Choose Joy". It is just not that simple, well it is - and it isn't. We don't choose joy like you choose an item off the menu. It is more like you choose to build your own joy. Choose the ingredients that are going to bring joy. Choose positivity. Choose gratitude and *"Do everything without complaining."*[36]

---

35. 1 Corinthians 1:18
36. Philippians 2:14 NLT

Choose hope. Choose faith. Choose time with Jesus because *"In His presence is fullness of joy"*.[37] Choose some worship music. Sometimes, for me, it is choose musicals. Choose to read a book. Choose to be present in conversations with your kids. Or at the water polo or football game. Take a walk. Have tea with a friend. Laugh out loud. Smile. Pray. Serve.

God also gives us a great tool to filter our thoughts and choose accordingly:

> *"Finally, brothers and sisters, whatever is true, whatever is noble, whatever is right, whatever is pure, whatever is lovely, whatever is admirable—if anything is excellent or praiseworthy—think about such things."*[38]

We can build joy into our lives. So yes. Choose joy by choosing to build joy. And when life gets tough, we need to get very intentional in our building.

If that describes you, if you are in a difficult season and having to fight for your joy right now, can I just encourage you? Keep going. Keep fighting. God is in this with you and He is fighting for you. I am proof that it is possible. Joy can begin to blossom and bloom in the midst of your toughest trial.

Do not give up, stay on the journey because it is all coming. Now, let's get back on the path, we are on our way to way freedom!

---

37. Psalm 16:11
38. Philippians 4:8

THE FREEDOM
JOURNEY

YOU CANNOT SERVE BOTH
GOD AND MONEY

"The Spirit of the Sovereign Lord is on me, because the Lord has anointed me... to proclaim freedom for the captives and release from darkness for the prisoners,"[39]

One time in high school, a few friends were hanging out at my house. My mom was not home, but we really did not stir up any trouble or do anything bad. We were watching *The Lion King*, and ordered a pizza. My mom called home unexpectedly while we were there, and when one of my friends answered the phone, she was not happy at all. In fact, she was livid. She made me tell everyone to leave and then I was grounded for a very, very long time. I guess I forgot to mention that this was the middle of the day, on a weekday, during the school year. We were all supposed to be in 4th period right about then.

As you can imagine, my mom stripped me of all freedom for a while after that one. Being grounded meant a very limited existence. No phone and no leaving the house except for school or work. Nothing makes a teenager appreciate school or work more than being grounded. The things I should have been free to do were not available to me because of the choices I had made.

Eventually the grounding ended, and I tasted sweet freedom. I was able to fully enjoy all the aspects of being a teenager again. Long, pointless conversations on the phone. Hanging out in the Taco Bell

---

39. *Isaiah 61:1*

parking lot until the police came and made us go somewhere else. Wow, I really did not use that freedom well. But I had it. All the freedom.

When I became a Christ follower, I also became free. Scripture makes it pretty clear that we are free in Christ.

"So if the Son sets you free, you will be free indeed."[40]

"Now the Lord is the Spirit, and where the Spirit of the Lord is, there is freedom."[41]

"And by him everyone who believes is freed from everything from which you could not be freed by the law of Moses."[42]

The original word for *"free"* means "to liberate, to deliver, to make free." Because of Christ, we are free from the bondage of sin. He has liberated us from fear, worry, judgment and condemnation. We live in God's love, grace, and mercy.

"Come to me, all you who are weary and burdened, and I will give you rest. Take my yoke upon you and learn from me, for I am gentle and humble in heart, and you will find rest for your souls. For my yoke is easy and my burden is light."[43]

It does not mean that life becomes perfect, but it does mean we should not feel weighed down by the things of this life and this world. We are free and we should feel free.

On this journey to joy, God showed me that I was not free in every area of my life. In some areas, what I felt was the exact opposite of freedom. I felt like I was in bondage. There were parts of my life where it felt like other things were in control and these things consumed a lot of my thinking and brought me stress and

---

40. *John 8:36*
41. 2 Corinthians 3:17
42. *Acts 13:19*
43. *Matthew 11:28-30*

anxiety and depression. They affected my surrounding relationships. All of that bondage was stealing my joy. There were things available to me I was not experiencing: freedom, peace and faith in God to be in control of every area of my life. Much like a grounded teenager, I was missing out on simple things that I should have been able to enjoy.

We are supposed to experience all of His goodness and all the good things He has in store for us during our time on earth. Not to mention for all of eternity with Him in heaven. But it is possible, while we are still here on earth, to end up missing out on some of those freedoms. Without meaning to, and maybe without even realizing it, we can end up missing out on things we should be experiencing. We wind up back in bondage in areas where we should be free. This bondage steals our joy.

There were three major areas where it was clear I was not free. The first was food. This was bondage that began in the 6th grade for me. It has been a miraculous journey of freedom that covers 30+ years. I am excited to share that journey. The problem is it would be another entire book's worth of information. In fact, I am pretty sure that is my next book, *Food Freedom*. My husband has even agreed to write it with me! I apologize if that feels like I am leaving a cliffhanger, but do not worry, God had other extensive areas of bondage in which I needed freedom. Money is the area He tackled first, and pretty swiftly, so that is the one I will share with you first.

~~~~~~~~~~

Some people get funny when Christians talk about money. I get it. But facts are facts. And I am going to present the facts and details that my husband and I experienced with God and money just as they happened. It was all quite miraculous and wonderful, but the path to get there was not easy or conventional. I am not suggesting that any of the specific things we did are exactly what everyone else should do. With prayer and wise counsel, we moved forward in areas where we felt like God was asking us to do crazy things. I certainly want everyone to experience miracles like we did, and I pray God would lead and guide you to your own miracles, just like He did for us. I believe He will.

After Paul and I got married, things were tight financially. After separately experiencing times of being debt-free, we now found ourselves with a good chunk of personal debt. Two becoming one and all that, and now we had a good size-able amount of dumb debt. On top of that, I had quit my full-time job in ministry to do my own ministry, and so there was not much income being brought in on my end. So, let's just say things were tight. Thankfully, my husband and I agreed about tithing and generosity, so we maintained our giving to our church throughout this season of having not much extra to go around.

We also believed in paying off our debts. So, as the one who was going to be in charge of paying bills every month, I quickly got a handle around what all we owed. I like what Dave Ramsey calls "the snowball method". Pay off your smallest debt first and then roll that monthly payment into the next smallest until it is paid off and so on and so on.

Our smallest debt was several hundred dollars. It had no interest, but it had to be paid off by a certain date or all the interest would be added, so it made the most sense to pay that one off first. I was determined. I began seeing every extra dollar as a dollar that could go to paying off our debt.

Unfortunately, with my personality type, this created a bit of a monster in me. And by bit, I mean massive, large, scary. Don't worry, you will see shortly.

At the same time all of this was happening, I was transitioning into this new family of five with my husband and three bonus kids. It had just been me and my little dog, London, for quite a while. To say it was an adjustment would be a vast understatement. The simplest things could overwhelm me.

One example was the dishwasher. We got married on May 3rd, so summer came really quickly. My husband worked mostly from home, so we had a house with five people in it most of the day, every day.

Each night the dishwasher would be full, and my husband would run it. The next day we would unload it and by the end of that day it would be full again! Well, this was just baffling to me. When I lived alone, I would run the dishwasher maybe once or twice a month. Most of the time it was just easier to hand wash one plate or a mug, anyway. The point is, I rarely filled my dishwasher and ran it. Now we were doing this insanity every single day. It cracks me up thinking back, but at the time I really did not understand. I said something to my husband one day about how we were filling up and running the dishwasher Every. Single. Night. He kind of looked at me blankly for a second and then slowly said, "Well, yeah, five people eating three meals a day means we are kind of using a lot of dishes and cups and silverware so I just run it every night, so we have enough for the next day."

It was probably the strangest thing he ever had to explain to an adult. And of course, it made sense. It was not a big deal. I was just learning new normals and taking it all in. I adjusted to our new dishwasher schedule pretty easily. With money and our budget, however, I did not adjust quite as smoothly or as quickly.

When it had just been me and London, I could decide to live on very little. I did not mind cereal for dinner. I could buy limited groceries and not spend any extra money for weeks if I wanted. London never complained if I was just home with him all the time. I had complete control. (Ha! Do we ever really? No, but I had the closest thing to it.) I could drastically cut spending without having to think about anyone else. Now I was a part of this amazing family. Now there were four other consumers. Four additional mouths with bodies to clothe and feet to cover and activities to do. Couldn't they be willing to just sit perfectly still at home for a year or so while we paid all this off? Please? It was a perfect storm to test my "in complete control self" and get her in a place of surrender to God.

~~~~~~~~~~

That summer we decided, despite the tight budget, to take a small, inexpensive vacation with the kids. My husband's work travel allowed him to accrue hotel points and the kids had season passes to the Six Flags theme parks so we drove to San Antonio where we could stay for free with points and go to Six Flags basically for free with passes already paid for. On the way back, we stopped to hike in Fredericksburg, Texas and enjoy some fun stuff there. A nice, inexpensive vacation. How fun! Except I had NO fun. Zero fun was had by Sara. Side note - If you had seen my social media posts during this vacation you would have thought, "Oh Sara, it looks like you are having so much fun!" False.

Yep, this is one of the genuine issues with social media. Many times, it is as fake as most of the eyelashes I see these days. So be careful when you see those perfect pics of friends and strangers and their "perfect" lives.

Back to the "perfect" vacation. I had one job to do on that trip. Track how much we spent and make sure we spent as little as absolutely possible. Sounds like a fun girl to vacation with, yes? By the way, no one actually asked me to do this job. I was self-appointed and empowered.

Y'all, it is embarrassing, humbling and heart-breaking for me to tell you the following story. I am crying right now just thinking about it because I cannot believe how much joy I did not have and how enslaved I was to money.

Important note: being in bondage to your debt is just as bad as being addicted to shopping and having a full bank account. If money has ahold of you, it does not matter how much you have or do not have. It is not about that at all. It is all about the ideas and beliefs in our heads. I believed freedom and joy were only going to come by being debt free again, and I guess I planned to suffer, and make everyone else suffer, until we got there. Not a good plan.

Any who, enough stalling. Time for the painful story I am dreading telling you. We all made it out of San Antonio in one piece. I remember a few tense moments around the dinner table as I oversaw everything ordered and every itemized check, but no one had thrown me out of a moving vehicle just yet. (Ok, no one ever actually did that, but I bet they thought about it.)

The Freedom Journey

We made it to Fredericksburg, which if you have never been I highly recommend going. It is a quaint little town with excellent restaurants and fun shops. One of those fun little shops is an old-time candy store. It has all the fun stuff you remember from your childhood, even candy cigarettes - Scandalous! And the prices reflect the same era. 20 cents for this piece, 35 cents for that. Perfect place for a low-budget vacation, right? All good here, surely!

Not even close. Y'all, I stood in that candy store and told our 8, 10 and 12-year-old that they could each have ONE piece of candy. ONE! Y'all, one. And I meant it. I was dead serious. And I watched them to make sure. Welcome to your new stepmom kids. Cinderella's gig doesn't look too bad from here, does it?

Oh! I am so heartbroken over that memory! I seriously cannot talk about it without crying. I just hate that I did that to our family. I made everyone so uncomfortable and tried to yoke them into the bondage that had such a grip on me. How I wish I could go back in time and yank that version of me out of the store and give her a good shake and say, "Snap out of it! You serve a God of more than enough, not barely enough for one dollar's worth of candy for three kids! So stop it!"

The great news is that trip, with the help of my hubby, was a turning point for me. I did not even mention the dinner we ate, where I found the cheapest thing on the menu and proceeded to eat my $3.99 pretzel while everyone else enjoyed amazing burgers! Y'all!

Sidenote: My husband actually swears, and really wants me to tell you, he did not even enjoy a *whole* hamburger that day. He split one with our oldest because he feared my wrath if they both got one of their own. Eek. Sorry babe! I owe you a hamburger.

My husband had seen enough. He waited until we got home, he had enough sense not to make the vacation worse by trying to talk to me in the middle of my budget brigade. He pulled me aside and lovingly said he thought I seemed to be struggling a bit with the whole budget thing. You think?! He was right, I was crazy! Poor man.

He was right, and I knew it. I realized I had a problem. I hated the way I was feeling. I was in bondage and I did not want to feel that way. I certainly had no joy. I was heartbroken over the way I had acted. I really wanted to overcome this struggle and find the freedom I knew I was missing.

I was not 100% sure how to stop being the money maniac, but I really wanted to try. That is one of the most amazing things about our God. He does not expect us to know how to do it all. We are not supposed to. He wants us to come to Him and say, "God, I do not like this, and I do not want to be in bondage anymore, but I do not know how to change. Will you help me?"

And that is all we need to do. We go to Him and confess and begin the conversation. Let Him into that area of our lives. Ask Him questions, study His Word and then do what He says.

God and I started talking about money a lot more after that. Specifically, He began talking to me about debt. Matthew 6:24 tells us that, "No one can serve two masters. Either you will hate the one and love the other, or you will be devoted to the one and despise the other. You cannot serve both God and money."

I had always thought of this verse in terms of loving to have money or the things money can buy. I certainly did not love our debt. But you could say I was devoted to it. Devoted to doing everything possible to pay it off. And the word used for serve in that passage also means to be a slave to. I was most definitely a slave to that debt. I very much felt in bondage to it. To our budget. There was no room for grace or freedom or an extra piece of candy. It was just a numbers game. And I needed to win ASAP and at all costs.

I do want to pause and mention here that the amounts involved are not the point. I realize that for many families not having an extra dollar for candy is a reality and money for eating out at all is not there. I do not want to be insensitive to that. The numbers are not the point, the condition of my heart in that season is the point. God's number one concern was seeing me be free in every area of my life and this was an area I had some serious chains. At the time I did think it was all about the numbers. I had no gratitude or joy for all God had given us and because of that I felt and acted like I did not have enough, even though I was richly blessed. I was far from free.

A big part of me felt I could not be free until our debt was gone. I could not have joy until it was gone. Once again, I had this idea that once I was debt-fee, I would feel joy. Feel the way I longed to feel but was always escaping me. Once I arrived at this debt-free place, I would finally feel all the joy that was eluding me until then.

As I let God into this area, He began to show me some things. One problem was the word "our".

Our debt. I claimed it as a part of our identity. I was letting it define me and us. And it led me to feel shame and guilt. "Our" debt was a blemish on our record. We owned it, therefore it owned me. God had to help me see it as "the" debt. Yes, the truth was it existed because of choices Paul and I made. God does care about how we handle money and we had not been wise. But we owned that and made changes.

Thinking of the debt as "ours" meant feeling that we had to pay for it and be reminded of it again and again and again. That does not sound much like God to me. He showed me it was "the" debt. He did not use it to define me or punish me or make me feel guilty. We had already learned from our mistakes. We did not need constant reminding.

Again, He wanted me to see that all the joy and freedom was available to me right then. He was not displeased with me. He loved me. But I had a lot of shame about that debt. I had been in debt before and had worked hard and learned a lot about money and tithing and budgeting. I thought I had learned my lesson. Finding myself in debt again was embarrassing and I felt like I had let God down. I felt irresponsible and like I was out of favor with God for as long as we were going to have that debt, and so it needed to be paid off as soon as humanly possible.

God can do more than humanly possible, as we were about to see. It is always better to let Him have it rather than insisting on our own way. He asked me to loosen the death grip I had on the debt and budget. He invited me to relax a little and let some fun back in. To trust Him with all of it. Even the debt. The truth was, there was a little room in our budget for fun and entertainment. I just preferred that every one of those extra dollars went to pay down the debt instead of enjoying anything at all that cost money. He was not saying throw out the budget. He was just asking me to add a little grace back in. Maybe let the kids have a whole dollar or two worth of candy next time.

It was not easy but I am also not an idiot, well not a complete idiot all the time, I was miserable. And I did not want to be. I figured we would try His way. I relaxed some and began to rest in His truth that

> **With God, guilt for our past mistakes does not follow us around like a shadow.**

He was not mad at me or us for THE debt. I could acknowledge that we made some bad choices that led to having debt, but in the present, we were honoring God with our money and our choices. With God, guilt for our past mistakes does not follow us around like a shadow. When we confess and repent scripture tells us that God "remembers our sins no more".[44]

---

44. Hebrews 8:12

BACKDOOR TO HEAVEN

All of God loved all of me. With or without debt. And all of His freedom and peace and joy were available to me regardless of my bank account, or lack thereof. One thing He said to me in that season was that there was no backdoor into heaven for those of us in debt. Wow. I had to sit for a minute with that one. Because I realized that was exactly how I felt. So much shame. And I wanted to be free, so my earthly conclusion was that it just needed to be paid off fast so I could feel *right* with God again.

It so funny how easily we do that. The Bible makes it abundantly clear that there is nothing we can do to earn God's love, His affection, His acceptance of us. All we can do is, by faith, believe in His Son, Jesus Christ, who came and died for all our sins. That is all. Just believe. I cannot earn it or work for it. All I can do is receive it. And I get that. But almost as soon as we enter into that relationship with God, we tend to forget that core truth.

It makes sense. It is not completely cut and dry. There are right and wrong things. There are ways that God instructs us on how to live. He does ask us to do certain things, even with our money. When we do not live our lives according to His instructions, there can be consequences to our choices. If I have a bunch of debt, then I have monthly minimums I have to pay to avoid lots of fees and even more debt.

Therefore, I do not have as much extra spending money each month. That is not because God is mad at me and punishing me for making bad financial decisions, that is just cause and effect.

We live in consequences for our choices, but we do not live outside God's love and affection while we experience those consequences once we belong to Him through His Son Jesus. But I was believing a lie that I was outside His love and affection. And being debt-free was my ticket back in. Thankfully, God takes it personally when we have wrong thinking like that. And He is always willing to help us learn or relearn the correct way.

I relaxed a little and found some freedom even while having debt. It was a journey, but it was becoming easier and easier. I tend to be a little black and white, all or nothing in my thinking anyway, so this was not the first time, or the last, that God had to bring me to a balanced middle ground. He is the expert at that, by the way. John 1:14 tells us that Jesus came in the "fullness of grace and truth".

Grace and truth. Jesus was all grace but He was not just all grace, He was all truth too. And He walked in the balance and fullness of both. None of us will ever do it quite like He did, but that is the standard He is going to be bringing us to.

So, there I was learning how to have balance and live free even though we had some debt. It was good. Pay stuff off, but do not be quite an ogre about it. Ok. I can do this!

And then, God.

Don't you just love those moments? You are going along just fine *and then, God*. And then, God throws you a curve ball and rips the rug out from underneath you all at the same time.

A few months into this debt conversation, I got the sense that I was hearing God say something to me that made no sense. I felt like He was asking me to stop trying to pay off our debt. "I'm sorry, what? I must have misheard you because I thought you said to quit trying to pay off our debt and that sounds crazy and so irresponsible, so I definitely made a mistake. Could you please repeat that, Lord?"

I felt like I kept hearing, "Quit trying to pay off your debt. Just make your minimum payments."

"Um, ok. Here's the thing, God. That's just crazy. That doesn't make any sense. See, there's this thing called a snowball and this guy named Dave Ramsey and we just - we have a plan here. Have you seen my spreadsheet? I have all the places where we owe, how much we owe, what interest we are paying and what order we are paying them off in. See how pretty? See the colors? And they all mean something different. I heard you about the relaxing bit and I have. You can ask Paul and the kids. We went to the movies AND got snacks and drinks just last weekend. And I enjoyed it. It was fun. I'm good. But we do want to be out of debt and in case you haven't heard if you only make the minimum payments then you'll like never get it paid off. Do they not have compounding interest in heaven? See, we have interest down here and it makes it harder... just trust me. I've got a good plan. Spreadsheet. Columns. See? Please?!?!"

That is pretty much how the conversation went. And I tried to move on, keep going. It was crazy! We could not just make minimum payments. What was He thinking? I was very confident I had misheard Him, so I told Paul what I had heard. Knowing he would say, "That's crazy. That's not God. We're sticking to the plan. We're doing what we're supposed to be doing."

So, I tell Paul. What does Paul say, you might ask? "Yeah, that sounds like God."

"Um, I'm sorry, what?!"

Oh, my gosh. What is happening? If I could have called Dave Ramsey right then to plead my case I would have. I honestly was dumbfounded. I was also terrified.

The next month when it was time to pay the bills I sat there at the computer, I still remember, I was frozen. I was logged into our bank account. It was time to put in the amounts we were going to pay towards our debts that month. At this point, I knew I had heard clearly and so I knew what I was going to do, but I was still so afraid. It felt so backward and so wrong. Like I was giving up on our goal to be debt- free. I realized though that I was not; I was just giving up on my plan to get us there.

It felt very similar to the story of Abraham and Isaac in the Bible. You can read all about it in Genesis chapter 22 but is it ok if I just SaraPhrase it for you real quick?

Abraham was an older gentleman who was married to a woman named Sarah, no relation. Because they were both old and had never had children, it seemed that they never would. Except that God had made them a promise. He promised Abraham that he would be the father to many nations. (We will skip over all the crazy stuff Sarah did to try and make it happen her own way on her own timeline. Again, no relation.) Eventually, God's promise was fulfilled, and Sarah gave birth to a baby boy and they named him Isaac.

Sidenote: the name Isaac means "laughter". They legit named him "laughter" because God had brought them laughter by giving them a child so late in life. (p.s. Abraham was 100 years old, and Sarah was 90!)

Sarah even said that everyone who heard about her having a baby would laugh with her. She thought God's idea about how to accomplish His goals for them was a little bit of outside the box thinking.

I hear you sister.

Fast forward several years and now God makes another crazy declaration that comes along with a crazy request. He asks Abraham to take his only son, Isaac, and sacrifice him to the Lord. It's beyond impossible to imagine. But this is what God asked.

And Abraham obeyed. He brought Isaac along with all the supplies for an offering and up the mountain they went.

They headed to the altar and now Abraham would have to be willing to trust God more than ever before. What I love the most about this passage are the clues to the fact that Abraham had complete faith in God that everything was going to be ok.

First, when he and Isaac head up the mountain for the sacrifice, he tells the servants that are with them, "We will worship, and we will come back to you." He believed they were both coming back down the mountain.

Second, as they are heading up the mountain Isaac starts to do an inventory of their supplies and notices that something is missing. He asks his dad, "Where is the lamb for the burnt offering?"

Hello awkward moment of the millennium.

But Abraham doesn't miss a beat. He says, "God himself will provide the lamb for the burnt offering, my son."[45] And that is exactly what God did. God provided an animal for the sacrifice and no harm came to Abraham's beloved Isaac. God was faithful.

So was Abraham. He believed. He trusted God and took what, I am sure, felt like a tremendous leap of faith and prepared to sacrifice his only son, believing that God was good and was going to provide a way.

Back to "not 90 years old and pregnant" Sara staring at the computer screen trying to surrender finances fully to God: I did it. I trusted God, took what felt like a tremendous leap, and entered only the minimum amount on everything we owed. And oh, by the way, we owed thousands and thousands, and thousands of dollars.

In that month and the months that followed, we only made minimum payments on all the debts we owed. It was one of the scariest things I have ever done, yet it was so incredibly freeing at the same time. Ok, probably not as scary as Abraham being willing to sacrifice Isaac, but still scary!

We were still in debt but I was completely trusting God and so I felt free, and I began to have more and more joy. I sensed God saying, "You worked very hard with me, and we paid off all your debt the first time you were in trouble. This time I am just going to pay it off for you."

It made little sense, and I certainly did not think that was what I deserved. I would have done it the other way around. "I helped you pay it off the first time, but next time, it is all you." Kind of like I have told our kids, "You get one free set of braces. If you do not wear that retainer and your teeth are crooked again, it's on you!"

God was saying He was going to do the opposite with me. And it was hard to receive. I did not feel I deserved it. But I did not have to wait long to see Him follow through. (To my kids, if you are reading

---

45. Genesis 22:8

this, wear your retainers! Until I hear otherwise you are still only getting one free set of braces.)

The whole minimum payment debacle happened around March. Paul and I had our 1-year anniversary in May and around that time we had occasionally had conversations about moving to another house. He moved into the house that we lived in at the time about a year before we met. We liked our house, but there were a few things that would really make more sense for our family of 5 in the future.

We also liked the idea of picking out and buying a home together. Nothing was urgent though, so we just looked at stuff occasionally online. Ultimately, we really decided that financially it did not make much sense, and we planned to just stay where we were for the time being. We had a whole discussion about it. You know those "discussions" you have in marriage? Those fun and a bit tense discussions? Yeah, one of those. We were not really on the same page, and he felt like we should just stay put. I said that was fine, I was content, but always open to other things, but staying put was fine.

Later that month, it was the Sunday of Memorial Weekend, it's funny how certain events get cemented into your brain, Paul and I were hanging out at home watching TV. Well, I was watching TV, he apparently was looking at houses on his phone. He came over to the couch to show me one. I was surprised at first, you know, because of the whole discussion about deciding not to move. Any who, he shows me this laundry room. I mean THE laundry room. The laundry room of my dreams! It was huge! It had lots of cabinets and a big sink and a window! I do all the laundry for us, which means I spend a lot of time in the room where laundry takes place so, yes, this was exciting to me. It also had a fabulous pantry. Side note - ways to know you are old - getting super excited about a big laundry room and/or a big pantry. But this house had both.

I liked what I saw, but I was not sure what was happening? Was he saying he was open to moving now? He simply said the other house seemed like it had all the things we had talked about. It was one story, had all the rooms we needed, and seemed to have more space for cars. We were only a few years away from more drivers in our home, and the current street where we lived was very cramped. It gave us a little more space in the house overall and checked all the boxes. I asked if we should go look on this lazy Sunday when we were not doing anything.

He said yes. It was in our area just about five minutes away, so we drove by to take a look. A very good friend of mine is our realtor, so I also reached out to her just to see if it might be possible to go look on the inside. She started looking into it, as Paul and I drove to see the outside.

We were actually not impressed. It was a little anticlimactic. Cute house, but it did not blow us away as we drove by. We really liked the street and location it was just hard to tell anything about it from the outside. We heard back from our realtor and in a few hours she would meet us there and we could see the inside. We figured, why not? We were not doing anything else that day. Besides looking at houses is fun. At least it is for me.

We went back a few hours later to see the inside. Boy, were we glad we did. It was amazing. It was so beautiful and had all the things we wanted and needed. With three kids, we had been looking at a hall tree for the entryway at our current house. Typically, those come with hooks and cubby space for two, sometimes three. We obviously wanted three. Well, this house had a built-in hall tree for three! I could not believe it. The laundry room, pantry, and hall tree were all right next to each other and that little section became my favorite place in the house.

As we walked through, I looked at Paul and said, "Are we really doing this?! Can we really do this?"

The house was a little more expensive than our current home, not by a lot but enough to consider. Especially since we were in debt and were trying to walk out financial freedom with God. It was a bigger house, a better location and had all the things but could we even do it? Should we?

We had both recently listened to a pastor give a message that talked about making big decisions like this one with God. To make a long sermon really short, the pastor talked about green lights and red lights. When you are facing a decision where there is not necessarily an obvious yes or no, try just taking one step in that direction and see what happens. See what God does. Do not get ten steps ahead, do not rush, but take a step and see what God does. If you have ever bought or sold a home then you know, it is an enormous machine with lots of moving parts. It takes so much faith to buy a house. There are so many variables and factors in play. So many people making decisions. I had seen God move in big ways in real estate transactions in my life.

We took a step to see what God would do. We prayed God would guide our steps and if this was not meant to be our next step, He would close the door and we would not force it. We would trust Him all the way. We were content to stay put, but if God wanted to somehow give us this house; we wanted it.

Our realtor reached out to the realtor selling the house to see first if they would even be interested in our offer. We would have to wait to sell our house to even be able to buy theirs.

Later that week, we learned they would in fact be interested. They had been trying to sell the house for a very long time. The owners had already moved out of state and had been renting out the house for a year and were now trying to sell it again. They were eager, which was good for us. Their realtor came to see our house to make sure she felt it would sell quickly. Here is where it pays to have a tidy husband and wife team who really like to keep a clean home. Our house was pretty much ready to list.

Plus, it had only been lived in for a few years and was newer than the one we were buying, so it looked great. Their realtor felt ours would sell quickly, so our first step seemed to be a successful one.

The really fun part was that we had already planned to go visit friends and family in Michigan, where my husband is from, for a few weeks that June. The trip was just a few weeks away. We talked about whether or not we should cancel the trip. Ultimately, we decided to go ahead and go. It would be easier showing the house with us all gone, anyway. Everything could be vacuumed and cleaned up once and then done for a while. We staged the house for showings, and the five of us hopped a plane to Michigan. Thank you air miles!

So far we seemed to be getting green lights. And the green lights continued by way of an offer on our home while we were still in Michigan. Thank goodness for technology and fax machines. We were able to do all the necessary paperwork from afar and it did not interrupt too much of our vacation.

By the time we got home, we were seeing tons of green lights. Everything was moving forward. Financing is always the most enjoyable part of the house buying process, don't you think? I know you can't hear sarcasm in a book, but please try. Financing is the WORST part of the house buying process. This was the one area where we were not sure exactly what was going to happen.

Basically, on paper things looked a little tight to the money people. Based on our budget we knew we were not biting off more than we could chew but the debt ratio blah blah blah was not doing us any favors. There were two banks looking at everything. The one we thought we were moving forward with ultimately came back said we could not do it. I was so disappointed. It felt like all our green lights were starting to turn red. Or at the very least, some shade of yellow. But this other banker guy -he was still in it with us and assured us it was all good, it was going to happen. And it did. I will not bore you with any more details except the most important ones, and the point to this whole story. With what we were making on selling our current house, we were able to put down what was needed on the new house. And we were going to get a significant amount back from the sale of our original house when it was all said and done. What? Yep. For some reason, only housing banking people understand we could only put down a certain amount on the new house. The rest was coming back to us. Here is the best part. It might even be worth giving a little drumroll on your desk or your leg. Go ahead. I'll wait.

The amount of money we ended up getting back from the sale of the smaller, less expensive house equaled a little more than what we owed in all the dumb debt! AND, the amount we were going to be saving in all of those monthly debt payments was exactly the amount that our mortgage was going to increase by. So bigger, more expensive house, no more debt and the monthly budget does not change. At. All.

We could not believe it. It did not make any sense. It was all God. Do you know how I really know it was God? The original banker, the one who said we could not do it with them, called our realtor after it was all said and done and said how? How did the second bank do it? What did they end up doing? Our realtor called me and asked me the same questions. I laughed and said honestly; "I don't know. I just believe this was our house, and this was God's plan, and nothing was going to stand in the way."

I am super proud to say that we were faithful once we got the money too. We tithed, we paid off all our credit card debt, and it left us with a little leftover that we were going to do a few things around the house with. Or so we thought.

After we had the money and had paid everything off, Paul and I were talking one morning in our beautiful new home. We both had forgotten one thing. Years earlier there was a debt - long story short - Paul's mom had been helping pay it off for him. And guess what? The amount owed was the amount we had left over. Well, that was not rocket science. It was the hardest part because we had gotten excited about doing a couple of things at the house, but we both knew there was no other option to consider. The rest of the money would wipe out that debt as well. Once our minds were set, the joy for the decision quickly set in. It was the right thing and it felt so good. The best part was calling my mother-in-law and inviting her over one morning and letting her know what we were doing. It was so fun! God wiped out all of our debt, all the while giving us a bigger home we absolutely loved and leaving our budget the exact same.

Now as I sit here just five short years later, I am in awe of all that God has done in the area of finances in our lives. The only debt we owe now is our home mortgage. We have money in the bank for savings, which we never had before. We have been able to be generous in so many ways and it has been so fun. I get why God is a generous God. It feels good to give. We have been able to take part in helping fund the vision of the church we love. And we have enjoyed time as a family on vacations where I actually have fun and do not watch like a hawk over every nickel and dime we spend. God has taught us how to be wise and live within our means and honor Him with what He gives us.

God has given me freedom in this area. It started out so differently. I was in so much bondage it does not seem possible to be where I am today. That is the freedom God offers us in every area of life.

Guess what comes with that freedom? Joy. Unexplainable, indescribable JOY. From the very first moment I began trusting God with our finances, my joy started to grow. I was able to experience joy in a season of debt and having very little, and I have been able to experience joy along the way as He miraculously paid our debt off and as He has blessed us financially in recent years. That is what I love most about the journey. Joy came first. It came before the debt was gone, before the new house was purchased and before we had money in the bank. And if it were all gone tomorrow, I am confident my joy would still be here. I did not find the joy in being debt-free or in having extra money - because that comes and goes. He taught me my joy comes from Him and He never changes. He is always increasing and never decreasing.

Joy came first.

Where there are areas of bondage there will be no joy. When we surrender those areas to Him, He will bring us into freedom and joy.

Since I am free from all the worry and all the anxiety and fear, I am free to enJOY all the moments. Enjoy the experiences. Enjoy the laughter of our kids. Just be still and enjoy what God has blessed us with. My friend, it is so worth it.

FREEDOM FROM DEPRESSION

Another editorial comment before we proceed. I am not an expert on depression. I am not an expert on Christians with depression. Not even close. I would never presume to know how depression works in other people or how best to find healing for someone else. What I am an expert on is depression in Sara Evelyn Shields Chapple. I am a Christian who loves the Lord and His Word fiercely. And I have also battled depression. All those things have been true at the same time. I have been delivered from depression a few different times, a few different ways and one final way. I know exactly how depression has been overcome in my own life. I would like to share those truths now without it seeming like I am prescribing any of that to anyone else.

As believers we are called to share our stories. In Acts 1:8, Jesus calls us to be witnesses. A witness is simply someone who tells what they have seen, what they have experienced. We are not called to be 'expert' witnesses, the ones who have all the answers, all the information available on a topic. We are not called to be the lawyers, asking all the tough questions, trying to prove a point or get to the bottom of something. We are not called to be the judge, weighing everyone else's answers, deciding what is fair or unfair. And we certainly are not called to be the jury, deciding everyone's fate, guilty or innocent. Just a witness. But a witness is so powerful! What I personally saw and experienced cannot be refuted. It is my experience. My testimony.

That is what I would like to share with you when it comes to depression. My witness testimony to my own personal experience. My hope, prayer and belief is that God can take these words and use them to speak to you and bring truth and healing to you. He is the only thing I would definitely prescribe without hesitation. I know He can speak specifically to every area of your heart, guide you in specific ways and walk you to complete healing in Jesus' name.

The Bit I Did Not Want to Write

I would like to skip this next part. Remember how I said I bring it all out into the open? It is true. I consider myself an open book about almost anything. And not that I am ashamed or that I have not shared the facts about any of this next part before. I guess it is the black and white on paper part. I have verbally shared pretty much all of this. But I have never written (or typed) it out before. I guess that is the difference. Spoken words are there one second and, in a sense, gone as the sound fades. Written down is written down for good. I have to stare at it and sit with it as I type. So, I am stalling even as I write this.

Avoiding telling you what I feel God nudging me to tell - that I know about the deep, dark places.

I have been to the deep, dark places of depression. I have been afraid of thoughts in my own mind. I have imagined sickness and disease coming to take me. Car crashes and accidents. I have wanted to die. I have wished to die. I have prayed to die. And once, I tried to die. I have been to the dark places.

I have felt the depths of despair and loneliness and hopelessness. When it seems as if there is nothing good coming ever again. Nothing at all to look forward to. No point to any of it at all. I have been to the dark places.

I have imagined escaping and running away. Leaving the city, state and country. Imagining the right timing and then just walking away. I have been to the deep, dark places.

I am fighting the tears as I sit at my computer and write tonight. Because as I sit here, my home is filled with the sounds of three amazing teenagers making a mess in the kitchen, chatting about their day with their dad and watching *The Flash* on television. They fill my home with life. And I am full of hope, joy and expectancy. But it has not always been that way.

I think the first time I really experienced depression was in the season I mentioned before, in the 6th grade. There was so much that happened in a short amount of time, and it just became too much.

It was in this season I first became introduced to the idea of counseling. It started with the counselor at my elementary school, and then eventually I was seeing a private one as well. I think that is part of the reason I am the open book I am today. I learned at an early age to open up and spill it.

I believe the counseling, coupled with eventually making friends in school, helped pull me out of that first dark place in the 6th grade. I know God was behind all the good that came into my life in that season even though I did not know it at the time.

The next couple of times I found myself in the deep depths of depression, once in high school and twice in college, I was able to come out of those low points with counseling and medication. My faith still was not a big part of my life, so God did not really factor into anything like that at the time.

The last time I battled depression in college was definitely the lowest point of my life. It was my senior year, I was living alone and not by choice. I wanted to have roommates, but it just never seemed to work out that I was a part of a group that ended up living together. I struggled with feeling left out and alone. I was also battling my eating disorder that was ruling my life. I was obsessed with controlling my weight, and I always felt like I was failing at that. Graduation was looming and life felt so overwhelming. I met a guy and we dated for a season, and then he ended things. I was so broken already that rejection felt like too much to overcome.

After a night of very heavy drinking, I got some food and went home. I ate and then made myself sick. It was a ritual and habit I repeated almost daily at that point. But that night I felt so tired of it all. My life felt completely out of control and I did not know how to stop it. I was so tired. So sick. And so sick and tired of being sick and tired. I felt utterly alone.

Whether or not it looked like it from the outside, I believed in God. I prayed often, but it always felt one sided. I did not think He really heard me. I did not think God was really with me.

God was in heaven. Heaven sounded like such a peaceful place from what I had heard. No more suffering. No more sadness. No more depression. No more rejection. So in my wreck of an emotional state that night, I decided heaven was really where I wanted to be. I just did not want to feel all that I was feeling anymore.

I decided to take my life so I could go to heaven. I took every pill I could find in my apartment. I figured that, coupled with the alcohol in my system, should do the trick. I wrote my mom a note and then I waited.

While I waited, I was actually quite calm. My mind wandered and I thought back to a boy I went to high school with. A boy who took his own life when we were only sixteen-years-old. It was a shocking experience to say the least. He had very recently come out of a romantic relationship, and everyone assumed that was the reason he had taken his life.

It was in that moment that I realized how incredibly wrong we all were. I think he was suffering for so much longer than any of us ever knew. I think he was hurting in ways that no one ever saw. The timing was what it was, but I really do not believe he did it just because of the breakup. As strange as it might sound, it made me wonder what people would think when I was gone. It seemed like they would probably assume it was because of the recently ended relationship. Might sound silly, but I did not want people to think that. I did not want my ex to think that either. For whatever reason, those thoughts sobered me up. Suddenly, I did not want to go out like this. I did not want it to be this way. I ran to throw up everything

I had taken, but when I did there was nothing there. I do not know if God intervened and I would have been okay, but in the moment I panicked and took myself to the emergency room. I had to drink a horrible concoction to soak up anything that might have been there and then I had to reach out to friends to come pick me up because they would not let me leave on my own. I told my friends I had alcohol poisoning and left it at that.

The next day I was not sure what to do. It felt tempting to just keep going like nothing had happened, but I feared what a next time might bring. I sought help through my university, where I was placed on some strong medication to combat the depression. This medicine completely took away my appetite, which at the time made me feel like my eating disorder was gone. Unfortunately, it was just masked for a season. I was able to pick myself up enough to keep going, to graduate, and move on to the next season of my life.

Fast forward to my mid-twenties when I was finally walking with God. Life was different, and so much better for sure. I was learning about who God was and who He said I was. He was filling my life with incredible people who loved the Lord and loved me. I was no longer abusing alcohol and I was learning to love my body and find healing in my relationship with food. But to my shock, and honestly, many times to my great frustration, I still battled this cycle of depression.

Inevitably it seemed to come and make itself right at home in me and there did not seem to be anything I could do to stop it. Once it was there, I would do the things I learned to do. I would get through the hard times and come out the other side. But the cycle always came.

Even after getting married, I still found myself battling depression. I was missing out on my own life. Now I had all this new life with new people, and the missing out became even more obvious.

When I was single, I could hide for a few days or weeks, and the life I was missing out on was not super obvious. Now that so much of my life was in my home with me, in the form of my family, it made it painfully obvious when I was in a dark place that cut me off from the people I loved. Depression was stealing from me. I did the things I knew to do - counseling and seasons of medication - until I found temporary relief.

As God and I embarked on this joy journey, He showed me some truths about my depression patterns that would change my life, for the better, forever.

The Broken Thinking of Depression

Have you ever heard of Yo-Yo dieting? It is basically when someone loses weight on a diet, gains that weight back, loses it again on the same or a different diet and then gains and loses, gains and loses. It is a vicious cycle that so many can relate to, including myself. That cycle, the ups and downs, the constant turnstile - that was my journey and experience with depression.

Since becoming a married woman and stepmom, I have developed a lot of new skills. I have grown in many ways. One area where I have a grown a ton is grilling. Yes, grilling. Before knowing my husband and being married, I had never grilled a thing unless we count my George Foreman and we really should not count that. I would not even have dared to turn on a grill, let alone cook anything on it when I was single. But my husband has taught me all he knows. Thanks to him, I grill our dinner regularly. I just love the flavor.

One important piece of grilling though, is the cleanup. After grilling, you get a layer of grease splatter all around the beautiful stainless steel grill. Each time you grill, you should really take the time to completely clean and wipe off all the areas that have grease splatter. Sometimes I do this and sometimes I do not. But if you wipe it down every time, it never builds up and your grill stays beautiful and clean.

When you do not take care of that first layer, you allow subsequent layers to build up, layer upon layer, and end up with a big mess and a big job. Now you need to bring out the big guns. You need more than just a wet towel. You need some chemicals and probably some gloves. And if you really let it go for too long, you end up in yard clothes with the hose and a bucket full of suds in order to get the grill clean again. Yes, that was me.

And if you do not do any of that, you could end up with a serious grease fire that could destroy the whole lot.

That's how depression works in my life. Hear me out.

When something hard comes into my life - an unexpected disappointment, something sad or difficult, it is like that first layer of grease. I need to process what has happened with God and with godly relationships in my life. I need some healing and whatever else God shows me I need so I can move on as the whole and healthy daughter He created me to be.

If I do not take care of that initial layer, then when the next layer comes because of another tragedy or difficult circumstance, now I have two layers and it is harder to get back to square one. It can still be done, but it takes some intentional time and processing with God; being honest about how I am feeling and what is going on in my heart. It is going to take a little longer now than if I would have just dealt with the first thing first.

If I let all that pile up without acknowledging what has happened, then more of life is still going to come. If I am not careful, I can end up with layer upon layer of tough stuff that I have not brought to God and have not processed with Him. I have not allowed Him to heal me and make me whole again.

When I have let too much pile up, depression can begin to set in. Or maybe I end up in a season where multiple hard things come all at once, and it seems I never have the chance to deal. The wonderful thing with God is there is always a way to get through the thick pile of yuck. He can walk me through with godly friends, and godly counsel from leaders and pastors in my church. And still sometimes it takes more. These are the times I have gone and continue to go to Christian counselors. These are the times I have talked to my Christian doctors about medication to help me clear the layers to get back to my real self under all the funk.

This had been my life and journey with depression. For so long it was a cycle that repeated itself, probably yearly. I would let stuff pile up without acknowledging and dealing with what was happening. Depression would set in, and I would let it. Each layer just came until eventually it would become too much. It would creep into all areas of my life. Affect relationships and keep me from enjoying life and doing the things I loved. Thankfully, eventually I would ask for help. Wise words from Christian counselors and doctors would lead me to do the things that made sense for me to do in that season to get well, to find healing.

And that was all good. Well, no it wasn't. But it was a vicious cycle I was stuck in. The layers piling up faster than I seemed to be able to get to the bottom of. I began this journey to joy with God, and He showed me there was another way. What if I could approach the initial layers of grease in a different way so I did not have to end up in the yard covered with soapy water scrubbing to get back to me? Or worse, end up choking on smoke as the flames of full-blown depression burned around me.

He showed me my thinking was broken because I believed this was just a pattern in my life that I had to live with. This was just how I processed, or how my family processed. Depression is generational in my family, parents and grandparents. Part of me believed it was just destined to always be this way.

But God said no. There was another way.

Yes, I could be predisposed, if I did not take care of those layers as they came. If I did not use the tools and do the things God was telling me. But He began showing me how easily I could sort through those layers as they came with Him and avoid the deep dark places once and for all.

In a way, it was like God was showing me how to go on the offensive with my depression. Let's talk sports for a minute. For those of you who were not born into a football-loving, Dallas Cowboys cheering, sports family let me give you a quick tutorial.

In a football game, the offense has the ball. They come out on the field, and they run plays; they decide if they are going to run the ball or throw the ball. They decide when the play is going to start and what kind of play it is going to be. They do all the initiating and deciding. The defense just reacts. The defense looks at what the offense is going to do, and then they respond. The defensive players chase the offensive players and try to stop them from doing what they are trying to do.

Until this point in my life, I had been playing defense with depression. I reacted and responded. I waited and saw what depression was doing, and then I made moves based on what was already happening. Depression was in charge. Depression decided the play and I acted like all I could do was wait for it to come and run me over like a 300-pound linebacker as I tried to stop it from doing what it was trying to do.

God showed me how to play offense and take control of my own life. I took the playbook out of depression's hand and turned it over to God. I did not have to wait to react. I could be proactive and run depression over for a change.

God educated, equipped, and helped me run the plays to overcome depression once and for all. Now I see my life and the things I walk through differently.

Here is one very practical example. When my dad died, I knew this was obviously a time of my life that could easily lead to a season of depression. I was of course devastated. The day he died was the hardest of my entire life. I am super grateful for my husband and family that surrounded me that day. I am grateful for my church where I could be surrounded by a family of believers all praising God around me. Lifting me up even though they did not even know I was there. We snuck into the top row that day. I wanted to be in that place I just was not ready for hugs, so I avoided all the people.

We have a family tradition of going to the movies together and as long as my dad had been physically able, he joined us. So that afternoon, on the day he died, when there was no more planning or arranging to do until the next day, I really had a desire for all of us to go to the movies. My husband, our kids, my mother-in-law and brother-in-law headed to see whatever was playing.

Now, in the day and age we live, we are blessed with the amazing new cinemas that serve you food. Those are our favorite for movie watching. As we all settled in, the server came around to take our order. I think I got some food, but the question of what to drink gave me pause. I sometimes like to have a glass of wine at the movies or with a meal. My husband ordered one for him, and I considered ordering one for myself. But the thought occurred to me alcohol is a depressant. My immediate next thought was, *Well I will not need any help in that area right now.* I made the conscious decision not to drink then or for a while because I knew I wanted nothing that could add to a feeling of sadness or being down.

Some might call that religious, but I believe whole-heartedly that it was the wisdom of God speaking to me. He helped me to play a little offense with the depression that could be waiting to set in at such a tough time.

I made another strategic decision that same night. I have a group of girlfriends that I have been meeting with for almost twenty years. These girls have been with me through thick and thin. We have walked through so much life together. And every couple of months we all meet for dinner to share how life is going. The day my dad died, we had one of these dinners already scheduled. My initial thought was not to go. I would just be a mess. My dad had died just ten hours earlier. But the more I thought about it, the more I felt like maybe I should go. These were my people, my girls. They all knew my dad. And talking about him and being loved on by them could not hurt, could it? So I went. And I am so glad I did. They listened to me, cried with me, comforted me, and prayed for me. Healing, in tiny, tiny bits, was already taking place.

Because of those decisions, plus getting to be in my church, that day was so filled with God and His goodness. I encountered Him and His goodness because I was proactive. I put myself into position to be near Him and His people. I continued to be proactive as I sought Christian counseling and met with my close godly relationships regularly over the coming months.

I was already playing offense. Running the plays that would help me and give me an advantage. And you know what? Depression never set in after the death of my dad. It is truly miraculous to me. It was shocking looking back months later and realizing I had not gone to the deep dark places. I had grieved. Don't get me wrong. I spent three days in bed one week (a few different times) and I was deeply hurting. I cried hard, I actually stomped my feet and cried out to God that I wanted my daddy. I sobbed into my husband's arms until I was too weak to cry anymore. But it did not turn into a scary, dark place. I just missed my daddy a whole lot, and I had to go through the process of grieving this enormous loss.

Freedom from depression is a group effort. It is not something we ever tackle alone. Me and God, my husband, friends and my Christian counselor are all on the team with me. But as anyone who's ever been on a sports team, or any team, will tell you, communication is key. It is up to me to communicate how I am doing to the rest of my team. When I am having a hard day or season I have to speak up, ask for prayer, or ask to go get a cup of tea. God has been so faithful in this area of my life, and I am so grateful I did not have to walk this journey alone.

You do not have to walk it alone either.

Ending the Depression Detour

It has been a while, since I have been to the deep dark places of depression, praise God. I fully believe by faith that I am never going back. I almost did not realize how much I was living with depression until I saw the space it left behind once it was gone.

What I want more than anything is to tell you, to tell anyone and everyone, God is with you in those deep dark places. Even if you do not feel it. He is there. And He has a way out for you, I promise.

I do not know what your depression journey has been like, or if you have had one. I do not know what you might be in the depths of it right now this very moment. But I know God is with you as you read these words. If you can do anything, please believe that. He sees you. You are not alone. I am praying right now that all the eyes that see these words will supernaturally become aware of God's presence with you. I am thinking of you, praying for you. The enemy really wants you to believe that you are alone and that there is no hope. Those are complete and utter lies straight from the pit of hell. You are never alone and there is ALWAYS hope. That is so vitally important we need to see it again. <u>You are never alone and there is always hope.</u>

The enemy wants to come in and convince us to give up this life, but if our life did not matter, why would he even bother? The Bible tells us that the enemy comes to steal, kill and destroy.[46] He wants to steal and destroy our lives. One way he does that is through suicide. But if our life really is as invaluable as he wants us to think it is, then why would he even bother? The truth is, he knows our life is of great value! That is why he wants to take it. He knows Jesus came to give us a full life. A life overflowing. And he knows that if we trust God and continue to walk with Jesus, we will get there. We cannot give up. If I had really given up, I would have missed out on the most amazing life I could have ever imagined. The enemy knew it; he knew all the good that God had for me, and he wanted me to throw it all away. Do not let him tell you the same lies. Your life has immeasurable value. God has a grand plan for you. I know it might not feel that way right this second, but sometimes we have to be willing to set our feelings aside and choose to believe what God says is true.

> *"May the God of hope fill you with all joy and peace as you trust in him, so that you may overflow with hope by the power of the Holy Spirit."*[47]

---

46. John 10:10
47. Romans 15:13

"Be strong and courageous. Do not be afraid or terrified because of them, for the Lord your God goes with you; he will never leave you nor forsake you."[48]

If you find yourself in the deep, dark places right now...
If you can relate to the idea of a cycle of depression like I described with the grease on the grill...

Please do not walk this road alone. No matter what you think or feel, I promise there are people willing to help. Willing to walk with you. But we must reach out and ask for that help.

http://anthemofhope.org

Suicide Crisis Line: 1-800-273-8255

http://www.christiancounselingcenters.org

---

48. Deuteronomy 31:6

YOUR FREEDOM JOURNEY

The freedom journey is about identifying the areas of our lives where we are in bondage. Many times these are areas where we are trying to have control. Ironically, these areas can be the places where we feel the most out of control.

Money is a big one for many people. Maybe yours is food, relationships, your kids, or your work. Joy only comes when we invite God into these areas, surrender our control and choose to follow Him, no matter what.

It can be scary and difficult, I am not denying that, but it is oh so worth it. I do not know how to convey it enough. God's plan for us is the best plan for us. He knows us; He knows what we need and what we want, and He cares about both.

> *"It is for freedom that Christ has set us free. Stand firm, then, and do not let yourselves be burdened again by a yoke of slavery."*[49]

Jesus died for your freedom. Not just your eternal freedom, but your freedom today. Your freedom from anything trying to keep you in chains. How do you think it makes Him feel to see us struggling in bondage? I do not think I am going too far out on a limb to say it breaks His heart for you. More than one of our kids have walked through difficult struggles over the years. Thankfully, my husband and I were aware each time and able to walk with them through it. It

---

49. Galatians 5:1

was so hard to see them having a hard time for the first time. It broke our hearts and we wanted nothing more than to take it away for them. But we were so thankful that they came to us. We were so glad they were talking to us and sharing what was going on. We were not mad or frustrated. We just loved them and helped them. We prayed for them and with them and encouraged them as they bravely faced and overcame.

Your good, good Father wants nothing more than to see you free, enjoying the life He died for you to live. A life of freedom and joy.

The areas of bondage that are stealing your joy and freedom need to be submitted to Him. It can be scary and might even look a little crazy from the outside, but you can trust Him.

1. In what areas of your life do you feel you are in bondage? What consumes your thoughts and has you worried more than anything else?

_____

_____

_____

_____

_____

_____

_____

_____

_____

_____

2. How has that felt for you? How long do you think you have been in bondage in this area?

_____

_____

_____

_____

_____

_____

_____

_____

3. What would complete freedom in that/those area(s) look and feel like for you?

_____

_____

_____

_____

_____

_____

_____

_____

_____

4. What practical steps could you take to release the hold on you? (Talk to your spouse/best friend, a godly relationship, counselor, pastor)

_____

_____

_____

_____

_____

_____

_____

_____

_____

5. Close your eyes for a moment and imagine yourself completely free and full of joy in this area of your life. Can you see it? Imagine laying down all the thoughts and gaining peace and quiet in your mind regarding this issue. Now ask God to make that vision a reality. Pour out to Him what you need. Share with Him where you are exhausted from trying to do it on your own.

_____

_____

_____

_____

_____

_____

_____

_____

_____

_____

6. Will you submit this area of your life to Him? Even if you don't know exactly what that looks like, it is okay. Just be willing to begin the conversation. He will lead you. He will guide you.

> If you do not feel ready to release it fully to Him, can you articulate why? What are your fears and concerns? What bad thing do you think will happen?

> Share all of that with God. Be honest with Him. (space available on next page)

I felt God asking me to surrender the area of food in my life for years. For way too many years. He would ask and I would say, "no, I'm not ready". And He would lovingly continue to walk with me and speak to me. He never left me, He never abandoned me to my own demise. When I was finally sick and tired of being sick and tired and ready to release it all to Him, He was right there. No shame, no condemnation, no "I told you so." Just His peace, love, freedom, and joy.

Begin the conversation.

Acknowledge the area and let Him know you know it is there; you just need some time. But as someone who took way too long and lost a lot along the way, can I plead with you? Do not put it on a shelf. Do not walk away. Do not wait too long. There is so much life for you!

So much He wants to place into your life, but right now there is not room because of all the chains. It is time to break free.

_____

_____

_____

_____

_____

_____

_____

_____

_____

_____

7. Go to His Word. What does the Bible have to say about your area of bondage? The Bible has a lot to say about every aspect of our lives. His Word will be an important tool for you in your freedom journey. (Googling "What does the Bible say about _____ " is a great way to see what God's Words says.)

   a. Money
   b. Relationships
   c. Food
   d. Purity
   e. Anger
   f. Authority

8. Freedom from Depression – If depression, or any other mental health struggle, has been or is a part of journey, I just want to encourage you to think about who is on your team with you. We do not walk this road alone, ever. God is always with us and He

has amazing people to go with us. Here are some questions for reflection for you:

Who is on your team? When was the last time you checked in with God, yourself, and your people? Is it time for an honest conversation and check in?

Do you need a team? Share with God what you need. Ask for a team to walk with you and then be proactive. Find a Christian counselor or support group. Talk to your church. Pray for God to reveal who your people are and with His leading and prompting schedule a time to share your journey with them and ask them to journey with you.

Who are you journeying with? You may not realize it but one of your greatest tools to freedom in this area is selflessly serving someone else. Are you on someone else's team? Pray for God to show you someone who needs you to walk with them. God will provide more healing down this path than any other!

_____

_____

_____

_____

_____

_____

When we find our healing in God and allow Him to set us free in areas of bondage, our joy grows. But our journey is not complete. There are two more crucial areas that I believe hold the keys to fully reclaiming our joy in Jesus' name.

WHEN THE ROAD GETS ROUGH II: *My Dad's Journey*

As I wrote *Journey to Joy* my dad was sick but, to me, he was not dying. I did not have an awareness that as I was on the path to earthly joy my dad was on the path to eternal, heavenly joy. I have chosen to include details of his health journey so that you can see how the events unfolded and how God was miraculously teaching me all these things at the same time.

I actually found it cathartic to put it all down on paper. It was a part of the journey of grieving my dad. I encourage you to do the same if you are on or have been on a difficult journey of your own. Spend some time remembering with God and look for all the ways He was with you along the way.

In the months leading up to the day my dad passed away, I was still writing and working on *Journey to Joy*. I was also journaling all I was experiencing and expressing to God my feelings on all of it.

I have always journaled. This season was no different. The combination of the two seasons, *Journey to Joy* and my dad's health, produced some very real and raw truths in my journal about joy in the tough times. Joy in the midst of grief.

I knew there would need to be a chapter in this book about joy in difficult seasons. I procrastinated writing that part. For a while the only thing I had written was, "Joy in The Tough Times". But as I started praying about what God wanted this bit to be about, I came across all my old journal entries. Leading up to two days before my dad unexpectedly passed away and going on for a few weeks after. I was so surprised by my own words. I was fighting. I was fighting to stay connected to God. I was fighting to stay grateful; I was fighting to stay in the game for my dad. I was fighting to keep my joy for him and for me. I think it is a beautiful example of the truths of *Journey to Joy* played out in real life.

First, a little backstory for you.

At the age of 70, my father was diagnosed with Parkinson's disease. With no family history of the illness, no one really knew what the diagnosis meant. He had a slight tremor in his left hand but other than that, there was not anything else you would notice. It mostly stayed that way for a few years. He started to shuffle his feet a bit when he walked. He moved a bit slower, but there did not seem to be shocking or drastic changes. We get older in our 70s, right?

Then in 2016 that all started to change. His mobility was declining to the point that those of us that love him felt he needed something to assist him, such as a cane or a walker. He quickly progressed to a rolling walker to get around. He was having falls at home and was struggling to do normal daily tasks like taking out the trash. Being the only child nearby, it was natural for me to start helping. I could make the time and so I started going once a week to get groceries, clean up a bit and take out the trash and recycling. My brother and I talked with him often about selling the house and moving a bit closer than the current 30-minute drive to me. That was a hard sell that never amounted to much. I do not want to say men are stubborn, but men are stubborn.

Then in the fall of 2017, a series of events began that would take the decision out of all of our hands and ultimately take me down a dark road where thankfully and somehow, I would find the joy I had been seeking all my life.

I was heading to the gym one morning when my dad called. Something was definitely wrong. He did not sound like himself. He said he thought maybe he had or was having a stroke. He could not remember how to turn the TV on. As he realized he could not complete that simple task, he began quizzing himself and realized he was not sure where he lived, what year it was or who the president was.

As I talked with him, I quickly rerouted myself to head to his house. He had a medical alert device, but for some reason was reluctant to push the button to call for help. No matter what I said he could not push it and at one point asked, "What button?"

After we had been discussing it for several seconds, I gently got off the phone with him assuring him I would call right back, so I could call 911 for him.

I arrived at the house just as the ambulance did. To make the rest of a long story a little shorter, my dad had a TIA or mini stroke. Thankfully, after about twenty hours he was back to "normal". The doctors however were shocked to find he was living alone in his home. Yes, welcome to our fun little club. We had been saying that for months. They wanted him to stay a few days for tests and then go to a rehabilitation facility to see if he could build up enough strength for them to feel good about him going back home alone. Thankfully, my dad was mostly agreeable. I guess the folks in white coats were convincing. But he was pretty determined he would be going back home after all was said and done. My brother and I were not so sure.

I began visiting and figuring out which rehab facility to send my dad to. Thankfully, there were a few options about ten minutes from my home. But choosing a place like that for your daddy is no simple task. The reality of our situation kind of settled in but there was not much time to process because there was simply so much to do. Insurance, doctors, getting what he needed from the house, taking care of the house - Oh, and did I mention hosting Thanksgiving?

Thankfully, my mother-in-law pre-ordered a turkey, so I did not have to worry about that. I think I made stuffing. But honestly, much of that holiday season was a complete blur. I am not even sure how the house got decorated for Christmas, but I do have pictures to prove that it did.

The week after Thanksgiving I traveled to Atlanta for work. While on that trip I received the call that my dad's insurance company said he was good to go, and they were kicking him out of rehab in two days! No one at the rehab facility agreed or felt he was ready to go anywhere. I appealed the insurance company's decision but was quickly denied. This is not a book about our country's medical or insurance situation, so I will just keep going. I flew home from my work trip with about a day to figure out where my dad was going next. After more tours and visits, a new home was chosen.

Since everyone at the rehab facility agreed there was no way he could go home alone, we determined he needed to transition to an assisted living facility. My brother and I agreed and now just had to communicate to dad. He seemed to understand he could not go home then but did not want to agree he was never going back home again. The move would just be temporary as he regained strength and mobility. That was fine with us, as long as he was agreeable for now.

Moving day was set for that Saturday. It all happened so quickly. A friend from my high school actually passed away that week and I missed the funeral on dad's moving day. I just could not see anything else except the situation with my dad. It all felt so immediate and emergent. I dropped and pushed everything else aside. It was overwhelming and crazy. There was so much to do every day, and I never stopped to process any of it then. I simply did not make the time.

December went on much in the same way. By some miracle, Christmas gifts were purchased and wrapped. Somehow, we had food and clean clothes. I know my husband picked up a lot of slack in that season. Right after Christmas, my husband and I, our three kids and my mother-in-law headed to New Mexico for a week-long ski vacation. Ironically, when we had been planning the trip the year before, we had planned on taking Dad with us. It was bittersweet since he could not go, but it was a great week for our family. I have always felt connected to God on a mountain covered in snow. I learned to ski as a young girl with my dad. Now I was taking my entire family on their first trip and seeing them experience it all for the first time. It was an experience I will treasure forever. A great reprieve from all that had been my life the previous two months. But it was all waiting for me at home, and I knew it.

As we drove home, I worked on my to-do list. We were in a detailed process of trying to get Veteran's Assistance for my dad to help pay for his very expensive care. I am so grateful he served our country, and grateful they offered assistance, but the process was anything but easy.

His house was waiting to be dealt with and rent to be paid at his "new home". I planned to hit the ground running as soon as we got home. A bit of sniffles on our drive was not going to keep me from jumping back into the sprint that had become my life. I had just come from my vacation, that was my rest. There was no rest time waiting for me at home.

When I woke up our first morning home, those sniffles had strangely turned into a deep and painful chest cough. I do not think I looked too hot either, as my husband quickly suggested I go to the doctor in case I had bronchitis or something. Like I had time for that. I have never had bronchitis, but I figured whatever I had, medicine would be good so I could keep going and get on with my day. A stop at the doctor and then I was on my way to drop off the rent check for my dad along with several other items on my list.

When I walked into the clinic, the doctor I had really grown to love took one look at me and said, "Oh honey, you have the flu."

So much for love. This woman was crazy. And I proceeded to tell her so. I quickly informed her I had never had the flu, or a flu shot - no flu had ever entered my body. I did not get the flu. I did not have the flu. She smiled politely and asked if I would mind if she ran the test, anyway. It would just take about ten minutes to process. *Sure. Let's cross it off the list so I can say I told you so and we can figure out what's really going on.*

She put on a mask, (sigh, drama much? It actually was drama pre-2020) and then she stuck some long terrible q-tip up my nose to see if my brain was still there, stuck it in some machine and we waited for the ten minute test.

This would not be a long drawn out, suspenseful ten minutes though. That stupid thing started beeping about forty-five seconds later. Flashing lights, bouncing around on the countertop and pointing at me and screaming "Unclean! Unclean!"

Okay, maybe not all of that actually happened. But it did beep right away because she said, all cheery behind her mask, "Oh, it didn't even need the ten minutes! Yes, you have the flu. Oh, you have the bad one too."

She showed me the screen "Flu A".

Whatever.

Everything sank. I could not have the flu. I did not have time for this. She said to go home and quarantine myself. But I had so much to do. Dropping off the rent check was now out of the question. Stepping foot in a building of elderly people did not sound like a good plan. I was not interested in being Typhoid Mary. I got my medicine and texted my husband and went home and proceeded to take the most shameful walk of shame ever. The last thing I saw as I closed the bedroom door was my husband feverishly and frantically wiping down every surface of the kitchen and I assume the entire house, even though we had barely been home twelve hours.

My world stopped. The full weight of the virus hit me that day and the next seventy-two hours were a haze. I could not believe how bad I felt. I had zero energy. When I finally managed to take a shower, I was wiped out for the rest of that day. *What was happening?* After a few days of this I thought, *okay a little rest and downtime was not too terrible, but it is time for this to be over.* I decided I was just going to be well. Ha! I think I made it until noon that day before I was back in bed sleeping.

As I was forced to stop all my activity and just be still, I was forced to deal with the state I was in. Not because of influenza, but because of my life and how I had been living. I was sick. My mind was sick. I was depressed. I was stressed. I was anxious. I was distracted and it was pretty much all my fault. I was worn out. I had no joy. There had been some pleasant moments on our vacation, but the truth was it was also filled with some irritation and frustration and overall feeling like it was not good enough. All the goodness and joy of the trip was completely lost once I got home. Before I got home. Somewhere on the road between New Mexico and DFW. It was like it all had never happened. My time in bed showed me how much I was looking at social media too. That seemed to add greatly to my discontent. Everyone's house was better, car was better, clothes were better, vacation was better. Marriage was better. I was resting to heal my body, and I was poisoning my mind the whole time.

It was all the wakeup call and reminder I needed. I was supposed to be on a journey to joy. I was supposed to be learning about having joy in every season, on every day. I was not putting into practice all I was learning. Where was my gratitude? It was being silenced by all the comparisons I was making to other people's lives through social media. Remember, "Comparison is the thief of joy." (Theodore Roosevelt) and it is not supposed to be on our journey!

I ended up taking a break from all social media for the rest of that year. And this was January. Seriously. I left it all. It began as a three-week fast that I did along with my church. There was just so much peace in my life without it all that I did not go back for more than a year. Once I did go back, I had learned valuable lessons about gratitude and comparison, and thankfully it has not been the pit it was for me in that season.

I got very intentional then, about where my mind and my thoughts were. How was my joy? What was bringing me joy and what was stealing it? I could not eliminate everything that threatened to steal my joy, but I could remove some of it. I could also be intentional about increasing things that were good for me, that did bring me joy. That is when I came up with the Joy Scale that you'll see at the end of this book. This was such a great tool for me in this season. If something did not add joy to my life, and I could remove it, it was gone. If it did add joy and I could have more of it - then I did. Of course, I did all this within the parameters and boundaries God has given us. I just mean I did not give into the sin of gluttony because

I felt like an entire box of Oreos would make me happy. There is no real, lasting joy apart from God.

My Journal

As I did these things, I got better. The joy came back, and it stayed. I saw the evidence of that when I read the words I had written in my journal in the months that followed. I'd like to share those journal entries with you.

Why exactly am I sharing these journal entries with you? Well, to answer that I have to expose one of the things about me that my husband teases me about the most - my love for the show *Law & Order* and most legal/justice television dramas. It is not an obsession but if you ask any one of my kids what my favorite TV show is they would all quickly say "*Law & Order*".

I value truth, integrity and justice. Because of that, I love these shows and I also love truth and evidence in real life. I can be a skeptic at times. So, I assume others are as well. I could see a book all about having joy and think, "that's a nice thought, but will doing these things actually bring joy or help me through dark times?" I think it would be normal to ask that question. I had to ask myself that question. If I am going to write a book and tell people how to live a life of joy I have to look and make sure I am walking all I am talking.

Reading through my journal entries is how I knew it was not lip service. As I wrote this, I lived it. With God's help and by His strength I put these ideas into action and I experienced the results. I want so desperately for you, the reader, to believe this is all true as well. I want you to experience the joy that God has for us. I want you to believe it is possible for you. I hope that by seeing the evidence in my life you will realize it is all possible for you as well.

I rest my case.

JOURNAL ENTRIES

October 24, 2018

Father, I am so grateful that dad gets to go to The Oaks. Thank you. I pray that he can stay there for the rest of his life. Thank you for Rhonda! And Nichole and Karyl. Jesus was never hurried, worried or stressed. He trusted you completely. That is the life I want, and I know it is possible. I prayed for wisdom with all of this with dad and you so perfectly provided. Thank you. My life is so full and blessed because of You! Thank you! I don't know what I would do without You, and I am so grateful I won't ever have to find out.

December 5, 2018

A journey to joy is just a journey with Jesus. It's a journey with Him discovering who He is and who I am because of who He is. It's joyful because I am never alone. It's a journey of faith believing that all of His promises are true. That the Bible is true, and because of that I have a life of hope and joy.

Calm delight. Finding true joy in the midst of all the struggle with my dad was shocking, but there it was.

I experienced calm delight the day he moved and when it was time to load him into my car, he was so weak I couldn't get him in. We were stuck in the freezing cold and wind. Me trying to hold him up, half in and half out of my car as the 3 movers came and helped me put my dad up into my SUV. Calm delight as I looked into their faces and tried to articulate gratitude to these three men God had sent that day to move him at the end of a long cold day but still had kindness and patience and love for my father.

Calm delight in seeing the staff and caregivers help my dad in this difficult season of life. It's joy. Not a jovial exuberance at his circumstances but a quiet, calm delight at how my Father is caring for my father.

I have joy in the midst of sorrow and struggle because Jesus is with me in the sorrow and struggle.

December 27, 2018

Lord! I'm really doing battle with depression this morning. I am winning though. Just the let down after Christmas I guess, and the lack of routine and structure the last few weeks. I could just feel it heavy today. I got up and showered though, cleaned the kitchen a bit, put on my favorite upbeat worship music and now here with some hot tea spending time with you. I do feel better. I know time with you was what I needed, but man I really didn't feel like doing all of that. Thank you so much for the gift of self-discipline and self-control. And for helping me use them. I need you so much, Lord.

February 7, 2019

So, what does the journey to joy look like in a season of difficulty? Of grief?

It's been a difficult few weeks with dad. Being quarantined in his room at The Oaks has caused him to decline quite a bit with his strength and speaking and eating/swallowing. They are talking about trying an inpatient rehab facility for a week or two to see if he can regain some of what he has lost.

I do find it a bit ironic that I feel called to write a book about joy in the midst of something so difficult.

I do find joy in doing the things I can for him. Helping around his place, cleaning, organizing. Getting the things he needs. Crossing things off the to do list for him. Just sitting with him at the hospital on Saturday while he rested.

I have gratitude for all the help you are giving me. The people you have placed around him who care about him. I'm grateful for Ron and how much he has helped dad and helped me. You have put good people around him. Thank you.

I'm certainly grateful for the life I have had with my dad. We've had so many great memories. We had a lot of fun and did a lot of great things together.

The joy is you. It's you in all of that.

It's being super intentional about looking for you and where you are working and showing up and providing and revealing yourself to me.

It's trusting and believing - choosing to trust and believe that you are here. You are with me and with him and looking out for him and me.

When I don't understand, don't know what's coming next or how this is all going to go, just resting in you, finding peace in you.

Talking to you. Finding and making time for you. Telling you how I feel. Processing with you. With Paul. Crying when it comes.

I am grateful that he knows you. Grateful he will spend eternity with you and feel real freedom from all the burdens that he carries.

Letting joy come how it wants to come in the midst. Paul and I watching The Masked Singer together.

Realizing and allowing things to be true at the same time - I am sad that my dad is going through all of this. I am uncertain and unsure about what is to come. At times I feel overwhelmed and I am full of joy and hope and peace and God is good and with me and he loves me and I am going to be ok. It's all going to be ok. More than ok.

February 10, 2019

8 am in the hospital room with dad

Where's the joy as I get the call at 7am that they are heading to the hospital with my dad again?

It's in the fact that I know You are here. You are in this. You are with me; you are with him. You go before us. You will and are taking care of him. You will put people around him. You have given me peace. A husband to pray for me and dad as I go. Dad is close by and the hospital is close by as well. Thank you for those small details that make all the difference.

I am grateful for your peace, your presence, your provision. I can trust you in this season, just like all other seasons of life. You are still good; you are still light. You are the light in the darkness of sickness, disease and death. I see your light. I choose to see it. I choose to see you and because of that; I do.

I could not do this without you. Being alone in this darkness would be way too much. Way too hard. But I am not alone, and I am not in the dark.

"This is the message we have heard from him and declare to you; God is light, in him there is no darkness at all." 1 John 1:5 ha, this just "happened" to be my reading for today in the VCC reading plan!

March 7, 2019 (three days before my dad passed away.)

You place before me life and death, blessing and curses, prosperity and destruction. I choose life and blessings and prosperity! Thank you for always giving me a choice! I choose life. I choose you. I choose joy. Even in the midst of all of this, I can choose all of that because of you. Thank you. I do choose you and all that that comes with it. Thank you!

March 8, 2019 (two days before my dad passed away.)

Something shifted this week. It started Monday. Gosh I was so emotional I could not stop crying. It didn't help that dad was not having a very great day. Tuesday was a little better, but Tuesday night was not. I could not sit in prayer and worship night at church! I don't know what worship will be like on Sunday. I am feeling better than I was Wednesday, yikes. Yelling at the poor woman on the phone. Gosh I just snapped. Then bursting into tears, trying to apologize. I can't believe how amazing she was. She was the angel I needed. Thank you, God, for sending her to me and I'm sorry I yelled at her. She was amazing.

She even asked me to tell her something, my favorite thing about my dad. I still can't believe it. Lora. God, thank you for Lora. Please bless her. She certainly blessed me and showed me such grace and mercy. My goodness. So much grace and mercy. Thank you. And after we hung up, I cried some more and then called the Christian counselor and messaged the girls for a girl's night STAT! Thankfully, we are getting together Sunday night.

March 11, 2019 (the day after my dad died.)

Gosh, there are so many thoughts and emotions. One minute I feel so peaceful because of where I know he is and then a few minutes later the tears come. Lord, I know he loved you and believed in you. He and his faith helped me be who I am today. And that means he is with you and will be with you forever and he isn't suffering any longer. I am grateful for all of that, but it is still hard obviously. I miss him, but I really miss before Parkinson's him. I am so blessed to have had him as my dad. We got to have so many good times together! All our trips. Thank you so much for giving me the life I had with him! It was such a huge gift to me. I am so grateful and proud to have been his daughter. Thank you for bringing him to yourself. Thank you for ending his suffering. Thank you for all the people who loved him and thank you for all the people who love me and Paul and are showing it. It does feel good. And thank you for Paul. It is awesome to have him to lean on right now and help carry the load of all of this.

Joy in this journey? Because I am not alone.

You are close to the broken-hearted.

You place the lonely in families.

I am part of the body. One part needs help the others help. Carry my burden.

Gratitude - for anything and everything I can think of

Movement - not sitting and wallowing. No isolation. I went to the beach by myself, but I was never alone. Talking to God.

Talk about it all. With Paul, Becca, counselor, God.

Smile at a stranger. I did that today and felt an immediate boost.

Do something for someone else.

Making a meal for Jenkins Family.

Not all day every day to the point of ignoring my grief or what I need. But I don't need to sit with my grief every literal waking moment of the day.

Let it out - cried for an hour at church last night and at counseling today, and I feel a difference. Feel better.

Thank you, Father for walking with me always and especially now. Last week when I just didn't want to get out of bed and this week where I feel more like being out in the actual world. Thank you for comforting me and just being close to me, allowing me to be close to you always. This would not at all be possible without you. It is going to be hard, accepting that I can't talk to him or see him like I want to. But you will get me through. Thank you.

~~~~~~~~~~

As God was giving me healing and freedom in my life, He was leading my dad towards his healing and freedom once and for all. It was not at all easy, but when I went back and read through my journal, I was pleasantly shocked at my words in the midst. I realized, I was actually doing it. I was putting it all into practice. And I was. By God's grace, I was. I was so intentional about being grateful and looking for God and all the ways He was with me and helping me. It made a difference. It saved me. It will do the same for you.

If you are in the midst of that difficult season, make the choice to have gratitude each day. Write it down. Keep track. You will see your Savior moving in your midst.

Do not give up. Keep going. God has some things He wants to say about who you are and what He created you to do.

THE IDENTITY JOURNEY

THE IDENTITY JOURNEY

"They will be called oaks of righteousness,

a planting of the Lord

for the display of his splendor."[50]

Before I met my husband, the love of my life was a fifteen-pound, white puff ball, Bichon Frise mix. I rescued him when he was about a year old. He was an absolute mess when I first laid eyes on him.

Bichon's have to be groomed. They also need to be brushed regularly or they get matted and then they have to be shaved. His original owners could not care for him and unfortunately the shelter he was in was a woman's home and I think she was in a bit over her head. He was dirty and ultimately he was sick with worms and some sort of infection. But, despite all of that, the day I met him I knew he was mine. He was so sweet. He was so timid but he came to me and I just adored him. In our first forty-eight hours, we bonded. He did have to be shaved due to fleas and severely matted fur. He had recently been fixed but the incision was full of dirt and not healing, so that had to be cleaned and re-stapled. He came home in the cone of shame and was so weak and helpless. He got around that entire weekend by me carrying him up and down the stairs and outside to go to the bathroom. That's how we bonded and how I came to love him.

---

50. Isaiah 61:3

His original owners had given him the name Torch. I was not a fan. It did not suit him. At. All. I had never seen a more chill dog. So that had to go. I needed to pick a name for him. I actually put quite a bit of thought into it and landed on London. I love to travel and that is my favorite city. I love so much about it. I love hot tea; I love the people and all there is to do. I love the Underground. I love being able to walk everywhere. And London seemed to fit him so London he was from then on. Bichon's are pretty smart dogs and he learned his new name quickly. I never called him Torch once. With me, he was just London. I got to name him and that was his new name.

We all have a name someone else gave us. Something is written on our driver's licenses, passports, and all the mail we get. Most likely our parent or parents decided on that name.

I was Sara Evelyn Shields. My name has meaning. It is one of those simple stories that ends up being complicated. When my mom was pregnant with me she, my dad and my brother were on vacation somewhere and a little blonde girl in pigtails was running around. Her parents called out to her and her name was Sara. Both my parents liked the name. There was one minor detail to consider. My dad's mom was also named Sarah. They had not really thought about doing family names. There were not any traditional names carried through the generations. Uh, except for Kermit. True story. Hey, Uncle Kermit!

It was not that they did not want to name me after her, they just had not thought about it. Plus, I had two grandmothers. Ultimately, they decided I would be Sara after my dad's mom and have the middle name Evelyn after my mom's mom. She was Jacqueline Evelyn. See. Simple but complicated. That's the story of how I got that name.

Here's the story of how I picked up another name. It was a time when we had family in town, I was pretty young, six or so. We were going somewhere, and I was the first one in the car in the garage waiting on everyone else. Funny, I am habitually early for everything. I guess I really was just born that way.

Anywho, as I waited, I guess I got bored, so I started singing. Nothing in particular. I think I was making up a song. I am not sure if I was enjoying the acoustics of an open garage or what, but I was singing pretty loudly. A relative threw open the door to the garage and started yelling at me to be quiet.

What they actually yelled was "WHAT IS THE MATTER WITH YOU??!! WHAT ARE YOU DOING? THE NEIGHBORS ARE GOING TO HEAR YOU AND THINK YOU ARE A CRAZY PERSON!!?! STOP!!!!"

That is the story of how I got the name "Weird". What I learned that day and in some other instances with the same relative was that I was embarrassing. I was weird. And my weirdness might make people think badly of me. And I learned that that should matter to me. A lot. Because it seemed to matter so much to them.

The truth I could not have known at that time was that I was just free and full of joy. And this person was not. My joy and freedom made them uncomfortable because they did not have it, so they wanted to squash it in me. Mission accomplished. I became a much more toned down, "appropriate" version of myself so that I could make others more comfortable. I let go of who I really was to become something I was not. I accepted the identity of shame that was never supposed to belong to me.

It was shame in who I really was and believing there was something wrong with her. And the way to determine if something was wrong with how I was, was to rely on the opinions of what everyone else thought of me. It was a pattern that would continue throughout most of my life.

Along the way in my journey, I picked up a few additional names that I felt described me. We all do. Life experiences and interactions with other people can and will cause us to accept and believe things about ourselves that are not true IF we do not know who we truly are.

Unwanted, unloved, not enough, rejected, not worthy.

I let everyone else and my interactions with them determine how I felt and who I was. If I was in a relationship and things were going well, I felt loved and worthy. I felt accepted and confident and good about myself. If my family relationships were in good places, I felt at peace and like I was a good daughter/sister/cousin, etc.

But when any of those relationships were out of whack, it rocked me. To. My. Core. I could not handle it. I know now that the primary reason that was true was since I was depending on all those people and relationships to determine my identity, if we were good I was good. Literally. And if it was bad, then conversely, I was bad too.

All of this led to some seriously unhealthy relationships, lots of dysfunction, codependency and pretty much no boundaries in my life.

I am not saying that we should not care when our relationships are strained. We should care. We should fight for peace in our relationships. We should forgive and ask for forgiveness. That is not what I am talking about. I am talking about being so distraught that you cannot function or think about anything else. It is hard to even make it through the day until we can make things right. Carrying the weight of guilt and shame and condemnation; always being willing to take all the blame. Believing that you alone are the entire problem and if you were just better, everything would be better. That is not healthy. And it certainly is not what God intended for us. We make mistakes, of course. We mess up and we own it. But it is possible to do all of that and maintain our peace, joy and our true identity.

I am also not saying that no one's opinion of us should ever matter. It's about finding the right people. We absolutely should have healthy people in our lives, that we trust, who can speak into our lives at all times. We all have blind spots and it's important to be open to hearing what those trusted people have to say. But let me give you one quick tip. If those "trusted" people only ever have corrections and criticisms for you, no matter how caring they seem to be, that is not a trusted person. The people I am talking about are going to encourage you, be for you, be your cheerleader and ultimately want the best for you! At times that will include sharing about areas where we are stuck or need to grow. But every conversation with this person should not be a lecture on all you are doing wrong. It's wise to filter even the right people's opinions through God and His Word.

At the end of the day, nothing that ANYONE else thinks about me outweighs who God says I am. He is my source.

> " At the end of the day, nothing that ANYONE else thinks about me outweighs who God says I am. "

It is not about trying to be or pretend we are perfect. Quite the opposite! It's recognizing and holding onto our true identity in the midst of our imperfection.

I do not want to be a selfish wife. But even when I am a selfish wife, I am still a beloved daughter. As a stepmom, I make bad choices sometimes. But bad choices do not make me a bad stepmom. My shortcomings and imperfections do not change who God says I am. Hallelujah! That is where we find joy. Joy that we can count on. Joy that will not abandon us on an off day. Everlasting joy.

The identity journey is all about knowing who we really are based solely on the words of the One who created us.

RELATIONSHIPS

When I really began to live my life for Jesus at twenty-four, needless to say, I had no idea who I really was. I did not know my true identity. I had never even heard a phrase like "true identity". I believed who I was, was determined by how I felt and how others felt about me.

Thankfully, when we allow Jesus into our lives, He wants nothing more than to show us who He is and show us who we really are. Who He says that we are. We get to begin a journey of transformation with our Creator as our guide. It may be slow and arduous at times, but He loves us too much to leave us the way we are. He will always invite us to grow and become all He created us to be.

This is the identity journey for all of us. To get to a place of walking in the joy God has given us, we have to let go of every identity that is not from Him. Every single one. We might realize we let them go only to pick them back up again accidentally or simply out of habit. Some of those old identities feel familiar because we feel like they have been with us for so long. That is why rejecting and letting go of false identities actually is not enough. Check out this parable that Jesus told in the Bible:

> *"When an impure spirit comes out of a person, it goes through arid places seeking rest and does not find it. Then it says, 'I will return to the house I left.' When it arrives, it finds the house unoccupied, swept clean and put in order. Then it goes and takes with it seven other spirits more wicked than itself, and they go in*

and live there. And the final condition of that person is worse than the first. That is how it will be with this wicked generation. "[51]

Removing the impure spirit was not enough. The space that was left had to be filled by something good. It is not enough just to remove the lies. The old identities, even though they are lies, still occupy a space. We realize that is not who we are, but then who are we? This step is so important. We have to replace these old lies and false identities with something. We have to replace them with the truth.

Any other attempt will be fruitless and could even cause us damage. I tried to reject the identities I did not like on my own. One method to replace "unlovable" was to get attention from men to prove I was lovable.

As you can imagine, that did not go so well. Unfortunately, there are plenty of guys out there who are more than happy to try and make you feel loved for a night or maybe for a season. You think it is working when you feel loved and you feel whole, but it is a very temporary fix. The problem applies to more than just romantic relationships. No human can be the one to tell me I am lovable because no human can love me perfectly all the time.

Can I brag on my husband for a minute? He loves me so well. He is thoughtful and sweet and romantic. He also pushes me to walk in all that God has called me to do. He is a big part of the reason you have this book in your hands. From the very beginning of our marriage, he has been encouraging me to write. Calling out the best in me and encouraging me along the way. As much as I love that man and as wonderful as he is as a husband and best friend, he is not perfect. And let's just be real, he does not love me perfectly 365. I am not revealing any deep, dark secrets here. I am not even talking about in our hard seasons, which we definitely have had or where nobody was loving anybody well. I am talking about in our best seasons. He is the love of my life, but sometimes he is selfish and not

---

51. Matthew 12: 43-45 (NIV)

thinking about me at all - how rude! But I guess it is only fair because occasionally I can be selfish and not love him the best either.

Even the best parent, friend, boyfriend or spouse is going to have off days. And that has to be okay. But if they are my source for knowing I am lovable, then they cannot have an off day. Because then my world falls apart because my source has been cut off. Their feelings for me cannot wax or wane. That is an incredibly unstable way to exist. I lived on this emotional roller coaster, laughing in the great moments, but feeling destroyed when we'd inevitably reach the very low lows.

When I would meet a guy and begin a relationship, I would live on cloud nine. It felt like all was right in the world. I had confidence and hope and happiness. But when the relationship ended, regardless of the reason, it felt like life itself was over. I would not be able to eat or sleep for days. It was such an exhausting way to exist. Up and down, again and again. Not a reliable source for identity and joy.

Some try to prove their value and worth through achievement and earning an identity through a certain title in their chosen field. Climbing that success ladder all the way to CEO. But what happens if you get the title only to find out none of it made you feel any different? And how many set out to reach the top but never get there for one reason or another? Will they ever believe they have worth and value without the title they are seeking?

When I started out working in full-time ministry, I did not have dreams or aspirations to, well, to do much of anything, really. I was twenty-four and did not know what I wanted to do with my life, except get married and have a family. As I started working, though, I saw my strengths and talents. I realized I was good at stuff and so did other people. I could teach and I started to grow as a communicator. I loved getting positive feedback from my leadership and my peers. I saw a path of achievement and advancement, and it was exciting. I had found my thing, I loved it and I did it well. Then God asked me to quit that job and walk away. *Um, come again?* That was devastating to me. My job had really become my identity. I was what I did. I remember even voicing a fear to my good friend that I was a little worried about my relationship with God. What if after ten years my relationship with God was so tied into my work in ministry that I might not have a strong relationship with God when I quit? What if I ended up sliding back to being like I was right before I started working at the church? That person did not have a strong relationship with God yet.

That is how much my identity was tied into what I did. I could not even see me and God apart from it. I began to understand why it had to go. Thankfully, my relationship with God was intact and more than that it began to grow and flourish in ways it had not before. It was a new season and a new journey with Him. It was a big lesson in who I was. My identity is not a church staffer, ministry worker, anything of the sort. My identity is a beloved daughter, and that did not change when my employment changed.

God's words are clear as we see Him speak to His Son, Jesus:

"And a voice from heaven said, 'This is my Son, whom I love; with him I am well pleased.'"[52]

It is important for us to note the timing of this event in Jesus' life. This moment occurred immediately after He was baptized and before He had done even one miracle. His Father loved Him and was pleased with Him, not because of anything Jesus had done but simply because He was His Son. His beloved Son.

Still others of us might try to prove we are lovable through our relationship with our children. The name of "perfect mom" or "perfect stepmom" will definitely let us know we are loved. Surely our children will love us perfectly all of our days. We gave them life after all! Well, maybe not technically in my case, but I make them food and keep them alive. They owe me!

But it does not take long to figure out our sweet kids are not meant to fulfill us or complete us. That will not work and it's super unfair

52. Matthew 3:17

to them. Even if they do accidentally do that some when they are young, they will eventually be a certain age where that will change. Not to mention we want to be modeling true God-given identity and speaking that back over them, not expecting them to fulfill us.

There are countless names we try to give ourselves, and we think all of them will be the one we are missing. We think we can find the replacement for names that hurt so deeply.

In order to find out who we really are, we have to go to the One who really named us.

WHAT'S IN A NAME?

Do you have any favorite family stories? Any famous ones that your relatives love to tell repeatedly? We have a few of those. My all-time favorite involved my grandmother on my dad's side. Remember Sarah? Well, her full name was Sarah Lou Oleta Cummings (Shields). I miss her so much. She was an amazing woman. She loved to travel, and she and my grandfather got to take some pretty epic trips in their lifetime. When she was in her 40s, they decided to take a trip to the Holy Land. Their first international trip. Naturally she needed her passport, so she began that process and realized she needed a certified copy of her birth certificate. Things were very different back then. You did not need a copy of your birth certificate for everything like you do now. So she had married and gotten her driver's license, all without needing her official birth certificate.

She made a call to the county clerk's office in the county she was born, out in east Texas. Once on the phone, she let them know what she was needing. A certified copy of her birth certificate. Sarah Lou Oleta Cummings born June 9, 1919. She waited as the clerk went to the filing cabinet to get the record.

But when they came back to the phone, they informed her that no one by that name was born on that day in Leonard, Texas. A bit confused, she confirmed the details again, Sarah Lou Oleta Cummings, born June 9, 1919. Again, they checked. Came back, no, there is no one by that name born on that date.

Thankfully my great-grandmother was still alive and ultimately my grandmother was able to go with her in person to the clerk's office to try to get to the bottom of it. Once they arrived, they were given the same info, no record. The clerk went ahead and read off the entries for births on that date and said, "baby girl Jack Cummings" and my great-grandmother exclaimed, "That's her!"

Now my grandmother was thoroughly confused. She then heard the following story for the very first time. The story has become family legend now.

Her mom, my great-grandmother, Florence, was born in 1902. She married very young, as so many did back then, and she had her first child, my grandmother, at only sixteen. Being only sixteen, she had a tough time dealing with her four older sisters, her mother and her mother-in-law when it came to choosing a name. This large number of relatives all had suggestions for the name and were offering them up to this brand new, sixteen year-old mom.

She had a home delivery and the doctor who was there requested the name from my great- grandmother for the birth certificate, but they needed more time to decide. He said he would be back in a week to check on mom and baby and get the name for the records. When he returned all were healthy, but still, no name had been chosen. I guess a combination of his impatience and the indecision from my great- grandmother led the doctor to quip that if they did not decide he was just going to put down his own name, Jack. The story goes that my great-grandmother offered a quick reply, suggesting that she did not care what the doctor did.

Well, ultimately the name was decided, Sarah Lou Oleta Cummings, and the words of the doctor were long forgotten, the birth records never reviewed.

Again, things were very different back then and driver's licenses were not essential, identification of individuals in rural east Texas was easy. As my Uncle Kermit said, "Not until World War II did country folk go off to the big city for anything requiring an ID. Even then, not until a passport was essential did the national government care. I did not need a birth certificate until I got a passport while working for IBM. All I had was a slip of paper from Baylor Hospital. Ah, the good old days."

Once my grandparents moved to Dallas, they could get driver's licenses and all they needed to do in life, without a birth certificate. That is, until my grandmother needed a passport.

What did my grandmother do when she found out someone had given her another name? Did she decide to become Jack? No! That was not really her name. The one who really named her was her mother. That doctor tried to give her a different name. He even made it an official record. It did not matter. Her mother gave her life. She was the one who got to name her, and that name won. My grandmother was able to go with her high school diploma, marriage certificate, and driver's license that showed she was Sarah Lou Oleta, and have her official birth certificate changed. That story cracks me up.

Can you imagine? Someone had given my grandmother another name. He even made it official. He put it in black and white on paper. The rest of his life for all he knew, my grandmother was Jack. But it did not matter what he thought. She had been given a name that topped any other. This discovery did not cause her to doubt who she was. She knew who she was, and she was not Jack. She was Sarah Lou.

It is so vital for us to know our true identity. If we do not know our true name we will not be able to recognize the false ones. If my grandmother had suffered from amnesia and did not know her name and all she had to go on was her official birth certificate, she would have believed her name was Jack. She would not have known the truth so that she could contradict the lie. This says I am Jack, so I must be Jack. They say I am unlovable, so I must be.

If I do not know I am loved and someone comes along and says or shows by their actions that I am unlovable, I will likely believe it. I have to know the truth to contradict the lies.

If I feel insecure and the enemy tries to convince me that is my identity, I will believe him if I do not know the truth that I am secure in Christ. He knows all of me and accepts me and lives in me.

Most of my life I walked around using names that all these other people had given me. I did not know that someone else had already named me, and what He said is what mattered.

Who my great-grandmother said my grandmother was, trumped everyone else, including her doctor and official birth certificate, when it came down to it. Who God says that we are surpasses everyone else when it comes down to it. That is such splendid news. Every other identity we have been given is false and has to yield to our true identity. We do not have to walk around not knowing our real name anymore.

Named

God named you, and He named me. And He has every right to. So, who exactly does God say we are?

> *"For you created my inmost being; you knit me together in my mother's womb."*[53]

He created us. He thought us up and then put us together. It only makes sense that He gets to be the one to choose our name. Names, actually. He has a lot to say about who we are. Here are just some of our true identities:

His Children and Heirs

> *"And I will be a father to you, and you shall be sons and daughters to Me," Says the lord Almighty."*[54]

Romans 8:17 says, *"Now if we are children, then we are heirs-- heirs of God and co-heirs with Christ, if indeed we share in his sufferings in order that we may also share in his glory."*

---

53. Psalm 139:13-14
54. 2 Corinthians 6:18

God has made us His children, His heirs. You are a child of God. I am a child of God. Yes, He gave us genetic, biological parents here on earth, but He was our first parent. And when we enter into a relationship with Him, His parentage and lineage surpass what we were born into. We get to have His characteristics. There may be things that run in our biological families, but now we are God's family and that has the power to overcome anything else. Maybe one of our parents struggled with anger and maybe they had a parent who also struggled with a temper. Some might say it is passed down and you are going to struggle with anger as well. But God says no. His character is what we learn to model, and it has the power to and will overcome anything that is not from Him when we allow him to work in us. Child of God outweighs child of divorce, abuse, neglect, addiction - whatever. This name that God has given us is above them all.

My husband's father is a wonderful, fun, charming man. He loves to talk to people, all people. We could go into a store and spend an extra fifteen minutes there while he chats up the cashier and they become great friends. Unfortunately, my father-in-law did not have the best experiences growing up. His father was an alcoholic and my father-in-law had to endure terrible things during his childhood. For a season he walked in the identity it seemed he had inherited from his earthly father. But eventually that all changed, and my father-in-law started learning new names and a new identity for himself. Ones from his Heavenly Father. It is a beautiful story of restoration and redemption only made possible by him letting go of the names that God says don't belong to him and accepting the ones that do.

The best part is how that is now carrying on down the generations in our family. My husband gave his life to God and let God come in heal childhood wounds. God provided freedom in the areas he was in bondage. And ultimately God taught him new names as well. Not the names he may have thought were being passed down through the generations. Not alcoholic, not abusive, not absent. But loved, known, accepted, and chosen. Because of that, my husband could be the kind of father his Heavenly Father was teaching him to be. Now he sees his children going even further in this area of identity. They are carrying on the new names they have seen their grandfather and father step into. It is only by receiving and accepting God's names for them that this is all possible.

Being God's heir means we get to inherit all the good stuff that He leaves for us. He left us so many amazing things. He left us His Holy Spirit and with that comes all the knowledge and wisdom we could ever hope for. The fruit of His Holy Spirit is love, joy, peace, patience, kindness, goodness, faithfulness, gentleness and self-control and those are the character traits we inherit and can walk in. I am a child of God, that is the identity He has given me and no one can take it away.

Loved

1 John 4:19-11 says, *"This is how God showed his love among us: He sent his one and only Son into the world that we might live through him. This is love: not that we loved God, but that he loved us and sent his Son as an atoning sacrifice for our sins. Dear friends, Since God so loved us, we also ought to love one another."*

Remember my absolute favorite verse?

"The Lord your God is with you, the Mighty Warrior who saves. He will take great delight in you; in his love he will no longer rebuke you, but will rejoice over you with singing."[55]

God says I am loved. Do I always feel loved? Nope. That is when I have to choose faith over feelings. I put my faith in what God says, not what Sara feels. And God says I am loved, all the time, by the Creator of the universe and the one who knows me better than anyone

---

55. *Zephaniah* 3:17

else. When I do not feel loved, I have to choose to tell myself that I am loved. It is not about a feeling. It is simply truth. God loves me. He has always loved me, and He will always love me.

Accepted

"Come to me, all you who are weary and burdened, and I will give you rest. Take my yoke upon you and learn from me, for I am gently and humble in heart, and you will find rest for your souls."[56]

This is big for me. I had so many instances when I was young of not being accepted.

Unacceptable became a name that was hard to let go of. People like to say, "Oh, I am bad with names." I say that. And I guess it has always been true. Once when I was six or seven, I was playing outside with a neighborhood friend and a friend of hers who was staying with her. I cannot remember the friend's name, which was also my problem that day. For some reason, I kept calling her by the wrong name. I was not doing it on purpose, I do not know why I kept forgetting but after I had done it a few times I guess they both got mad. We were playing in some water in the street because it had just finished raining. They filled some of the cups we were playing with and threw water on me for calling her the wrong name. It is one of my earliest memories. I remember being in shock and so upset. I went home crying and all wet. My older brother, remember Clint who I looked up to so much? Well, here is a great example of why. When I got home he was there, and I told him what happened. Initially, I am pretty sure he wanted to head into the street and return the favor, but instead he ushered me inside, dried me off and dried my tears. I did not feel accepted that day by my friends. But when I came home, a

---

56. *Matthew* 11:28-29

soaking wet mess, my brother accepted me. He brought me in and cleaned up.

We get to go to God the same way. He accepts us just as we are. We come to Him a mess and it is okay. He loves us so much He will lovingly begin the process of cleaning us up, He will not leave us in the state we arrive in. But we can always come to Him.

A Friend

"I no longer call you servants, because a servant does not know his master's business. Instead, I have called you friends, for everything that I learned from my Father I have made known to you."[57]

Of all the names God gives me, this one might be the most astonishing. I do not know why I went through so many tough seasons with friends. Some of it is just life. Kids can be mean. I can remember being mean to a girl along with some other kids in 3rd grade. I hate those memories. As I got older, I know I was a pretty needy friend. All the stuff I had going on at home plus the absence of a relationship with God just left a lot of holes in my life. I looked to these friends and potential friends to fill some of those gaps in an unbalanced and unhealthy way. I also do not think I knew how to be a very good friend. There were lots of reasons, but for a large part of my adolescent life I struggled to feel like the friends I had actually cared about me. So thinking that the God of the universe considers me a friend is incredible to me. Especially because He knows me so well and knows just how needy and selfish I can be. The original word for "friend" means, *"a dear friend, being fond of someone."* God is my dear friend and He is fond of me. Wow. That is an identity I would not trade for anything or let anyone take away from me. I

---

57. John 15:15

am a friend of God. Thankfully, over the years God has filled my life with incredible friends who love me so well and I have learned how to be a better friend to the people in my life. I know I've learned that because of the kind of friend God has been to me. I am so thankful to be His friend.

Worthy

"For we are God's handiwork, created in Christ Jesus to do good works, which God prepared in advance for us to do."[58]

So many times in life people and circumstances can leave us believing the lie that we are not worthy. I certainly struggled with that false identity. The truth is, other people may have felt that we were not worthy. But that is only an indication that they had an issue. The problem was with them, not you. In our flesh, we tend to want to make others feel as bad as we do. The saying goes "hurt people hurt people" and it is so true. We have been hurt and we have hurt people. But no matter what any human on this planet thinks - even someone you think knows you better than anyone - and so you give lots of credibility to their opinion - even that person, if who they say you are in any way contradicts who God says you are, then it is false. It is a lie, and we have to reject those lies and replace them with God's truth. He is the one who knows us best. He created us. He gets the final say. We cannot confuse behavior with identity. We will talk more about what we do and our purpose in the next section, but we are not defined by the mistakes we have made and are going to make.

If we were not worthy God would not have sent His Son to die for us on the cross and Jesus would not have taken our place on that cross to die for all our sins. We are so worthy we didn't even have to

---

58. Ephesians 2:10

do anything. We do not have to earn it. We just receive the free gift from Him, because He says we are worthy.

God says we are worthy to be called all the wonderful things we have already discussed here. We are worthy because we are created in His image and when we accept Jesus we "put on Christ"[59] and that changes who we are forever. It makes us worthy and it also makes us righteous because all of Christ's qualities transfer to us as His children.

Righteous

"God made him who had no sin to be sin for us, so that in him we might become the righteousness of God."[60]

"This righteousness is given through faith in Jesus Christ to all who believe."[61]

Righteous is one of those big words that carries with it wonderful meaning.

"To be righteous means to be in a condition acceptable to God. It also means integrity, virtue, purity of life, rightness, correctness of thinking, feeling and acting." – Thayer

That is a high calling. On our own, we could never have the name of righteous. Thankfully, we are not on our own. We are not righteous because we live righteously, we are righteous because He lived righteously. Then, because of God's grace, this righteousness is credited to us. It's nothing we deserve, and it's nothing we can earn. It is simply offered to us to receive. We have been given the gift

---

59. Romans 13:14
60. 2 Corinthians 5:21
61. Romans 3:22

of Jesus' perfect life, His "condition acceptable to God" and His "integrity, virtue, purity of life, rightness, correctness of thinking, feeling and acting." When you and I accept Christ, all of His perfection and right standing with God the Father passes to us and we become a new creation.[62] That new creation is what God sees when He looks at us. He sees Jesus. He still sees us. He just sees us through the filter of Jesus and His perfect life that covers all our sins. He sees us as righteous.

There are many other names that God has given us. As we walk with Him and study His Word, He reveals those to us again and again. It is a process of learning and understanding our identity in Christ. He has given us one powerful tool to make this all possible.

---

62. 2 Corinthians 5:17

THE MIND OF CHRIST

"for, 'Who has known the mind of the Lord so as to instruct him?' But we have the mind of Christ."[63]

You are what you eat may be a true saying, but an even truer one is "You are what you think." This is the area that so often makes or breaks us: What we choose to think. This entire journey is a series of choices about what to think. What to think of ourselves, our identity. Which version to believe in? The one the world, and possibly people we love, have given us? Or the one God wants so very much to give us? The truth is, we have been given a valuable tool to aid us in this area: the mind of Christ. When we accept Christ and His Holy Spirit comes to live inside of us, we gain access to many things. The Bible tells us that one of those gifts is the mind of Christ.

A few years ago, for my birthday, I received a record player. I was so excited. The kids each picked out albums they thought I would like, and we all had fun listening to them that day and for the next few weeks. But after the newness and novelty of the record player wore off, we played it less and less. Eventually it simply became part of the decor. After we had some renovations done in our home last year, the record player ended up in a new spot in the house. It is a little more out in the open now, and I have been playing records again. I love it. I love the experience of listening to those albums and enjoying the thoughtful gift my family gave me. I even have some

---

63. 1 Corinthians 2:16

old albums that belonged to my dad, and I love to sit down with a cup of hot tea and listen. For a season, though, I had been given a record player that I did not use. I never used it, so I never experienced it. It was as if I had never received it at all. If we are given something but never use it, we can never experience it.

In order to experience the mind of Christ, we have to use it. Another way to say it is we have access to the mind of Christ. With that access, we have the ability to understand His Word. We can change our patterns of thinking to line up with what Christ believes. Another gift from God is the spirit of self-control and self-discipline.[64] We absolutely are given the ability to choose and believe. When we know Christ, we have the mind of Christ. And that means we have His thoughts about us. So it just comes down to choice and belief.

More than anything, I think we have to accept the fact that our Heavenly Father knows us better than anyone else ever could. He knows our innermost thoughts. The things we would never dare speak aloud to our closest confidant, He knows. He loves us madly anyway. He knows it all, and He still calls us His, loved, chosen, worthy, accepted, righteous. It is our choice whether or not we are going to believe it.

The simple fact is that our joy will always be incomplete if we are not sure of our identity. Maybe a better way to say it is our joy will be unreliable and fluctuating. It will come and go depending on how others are currently viewing us, how we are behaving and definitely how we are feeling. Those are ever revolving doors for me; I don't know about you.

God's opinion of us never changes. I can wake up each morning and be sure that regardless of what happened yesterday, or what might happen today, who God says I am has not changed. It cannot change. I can and need to speak His never changing identity of myself over myself again and again. For as long as I walk this earth.

---

64. Galatians 5:22, 2 Timothy 1:7

True North

Why do we have to do this over and over? Why can't it be one and done?

Those are brilliant questions. I am so glad you asked. There are several reasons this is not a one and done exercise.

First off, we remember the negative more than positive. All kinds of super smart people have done studies of our minds and learned that we recall bad things significantly more easily than we do the positive. It even has a fancy name, the Negativity Bias. (Negativity Bias, Negativity Dominance, and Contagion Paul Rozin and Edward B. Royzman Department of Psychology and Solomon Asch Center for Study of Ethnopolitical Conflict University of Pennsylvania)

Various psychologists and brain experts believe it takes five to seven positive experiences or comments to overcome one negative experience or comment.

Now imagine all the times a false identity has been spoken over you and your life. It could have been by others, but also by yourself. So often we believe and agree with the false identity, and that reinforces it even more. Now we are starting the journey of undoing, unbelieving those lies and believing the truth. That will take some time and grace-filled effort on our part, but it is so worth it. Thankfully, with God's super-natural help, we are not necessarily bound to a 5:1 ratio. He can bring healing and restoration in His time. We get to partner with Him and do our part to choose to believe the right things.

We keep at it. We tell ourselves the truth again and again. We put ourselves in situations and around people who will now reinforce the truth. We become more aware when these false identities are spoken over us and we don't agree with them. We make the choice not to believe it, and then we reinforce the truth by reminding ourselves the truth about who God says we are. As a wise former co-worker of mine explained, just because a thought knocks on the door of our mind does not mean we have to open the door and invite it in for tea.

The thought might appear, but I do not have to agree with it. I do not have to let it take root to become something I have to undo five to seven times.

Another reason this is an ongoing process is because of a truth that my pastor likes to say, we leak. We hear great things; we believe great things, but slowly over time if we are not being intentional, those things can end up slipping out of us. This ties in to the last reason we need to be reminded of our true identities again and again.

Part of the reason it is so easy for us to leak is that so much other stuff gets thrown at us that competes with God's truth. This has always been true, but I certainly think it is truer now than ever before. We are constantly receiving information. We have so many screens in front of us all day and so many voices we are reading and hearing.

Truth can easily get buried, turned upside down and mixed in with other things. It is a constant reshuffling in order to bring God's truth back to the top and set things right again. It takes intentionality to clear away the clutter that makes it hard to see what God's truth really is.

It is like the decorative pillows on my couch. If you did not know, there is a correct way for them to be placed and fluffed. There is even a correct side that needs to be facing up on my holiday pillows with cute pumpkins at Thanksgiving and the word "joy" at Christmas.

I set the pillows correctly on the couch every day. My husband does this too, although inevitably at the holidays we end up with sideways pumpkins or upside-down joy. Funny thing, when the "joy" pillow is upside down it looks like it's spelling "ho!" No joke. But the pillows get set and then the day gets going. People, three teenagers mostly, come and sit and lay on the couch. When they do, they move the decorative pillows, which is a win, let's not miss that moment. They move the decorative pillows.

Which has nothing to do with this topic except that it makes my momma heart happy.

But the pillows end up on the floor or at the end of the couch or backwards or any which way except the way that is correct. Life happens and things get out of whack. So, I come back in the evening or the next morning and set things right again. Turn the ho! back to joy.

For us, we may sit with God in the morning and download His truth for our lives. His identity for us. And we receive it. We are set right! And then

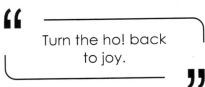

> Turn the ho! back to joy.

we go about our day. We interact with people. I start out knowing I am a beloved daughter, but then my husband is acting a bit funky, so it makes me feel funky and my true identity slips a little. We end up rushing out the door to get to school because someone cannot find something and I realize there is no lunch for the kids to take to school. Stepmom fail. Identity takes another hit. Once I am back home I hop on social media for a minute and see my friend with her flawless hair and makeup and I wonder if I am doing enough. Another crack in my identity foundation.

See how easily we can forget who we really are? And as the day goes on, if I am not reminding myself who God says I am, I can get to the end of the day and be completely sideways! Or worse, be upside down yelling "ho!", at everyone!

Jesus explained it with a parable in Matthew 13:

Then he told them many things in parables, saying: "A farmer went out to sow his seed. As he was scattering the seed, some fell along the path, and the birds came and ate it up. Some fell on rocky places, where it did not have much soil. It sprang up quickly, because the soil was shallow. But when the sun came up, the plants were scorched, and they withered because they had no root. Other seed fell among thorns, which grew up and choked the plants. Still other seed fell on good soil, where it produced a crop-- a hundred, sixty or thirty times what was sown."

The disciples didn't quite understand, so He explained it for them and us:

"Listen then to what the parable of the sower means: When anyone hears the message about the kingdom and does not understand it, the evil one comes and snatches away what was sown in their heart. This is the seed sown along the path. The seed falling on rocky ground refers to someone who hears the word and at once receives it with joy. But since they have no root, they last only a short time. When trouble or persecution comes because of the word, they quickly fall away. The seed falling among the thorns refers to someone who hears the word, but the worries of this life and the deceitfulness of wealth choke the word, making it unfruitful. But the seed falling on good soil refers to someone who hears the word and understands it. This is the one who produces a crop, yielding a hundred, sixty or thirty times what was sown."

We want to be in the category who "hears the word and understands it". In order for that to happen, we have to first hear the word. Reading, listening, and meditating on His truth is crucial for us. When we meditate, it just means we think about it. We think about scripture. We take our new minds and we use them the way God intended. When we do that, it helps with the second part, understanding. The important connection between the two is our belief. Taking these powerful minds we have received and choosing to believe His truth over all the lies.

The world and its lies are coming at us from all angles all day long. We have to fight to keep our true North, to keep ahold of the Words that God gives to us. To maintain a foundation that is based on God's truth and His alone. We can do it. Absolutely. But we have to be intentional, and we have to be repetitious. Unlike my pillow situation though, which will most likely repeat itself every Thanksgiving and Christmas, our process will progress over time. It will get easier. The false identities will be more and more obvious and easier to spot and swap with the truth. We will believe the new identity and walk out our lives based on who we now know that we are. But in order to get there, we have to start where we are and keep going on the journey.

Assessed

A few words on personality tests.

In recent years, personality tests have become more and more popular. Every few years a new one catches fire and becomes super popular. In the past it has mostly been in the business world and a little in the church world. But recently I have seen more and more talk and even preaching in the church about personality assessments.

I have a word of caution for us for all personality tests and assessments: It is okay to know our strengths. It is okay to know about ourselves. But the question we need to ask ourselves is who are we studying more? Who are we trying to understand better and know more about? Ourselves? Or Jesus?

The thing is, when I study Jesus, I learn about myself. As I study my Maker, He teaches me about how He made me and what He made me for. It's all on purpose. He wants to develop us and grow us.

It is important to ask, "Where am I looking, primarily, to learn who I am?" A manmade assessment based on who knows what? Or the Word of God, inspired by God, about the people of God, namely you.

The study of self will never bring us the joy, peace, fulfillment, or wholeness we seek. That can only be found in an ongoing, ever-growing relationship in and deepening dependence on Christ. We come to the Lord to know who we are:

> *"Search me, God, and know my heart; test me and know my anxious thoughts. See if there is any offensive way in me, and lead me in the way everlasting."*[65]

In Scripture, there is an incredible story about a woman who encounters Jesus. Many times it is referred to as the Woman at the Well. Jesus talks with this woman, and she soon discovers that He

---

65. Psalm 139:23-24

knows all about her and her life. He speaks to her about who He is and what He has come to do. He offers her a new life through Him. After her encounter, she goes back to her town and tells everyone that she met a man who "...told me everything I ever did." Many people came to believe in Jesus because of her testimony.[66]

This woman met Jesus and He told her everything about herself. We do not have to go on a path to self-discovery. When we discover Jesus, He holds the answers to all that we are.

He is the well and He never runs dry. We can always go back to Him again and again. There is always more to discover in Him. As we learn more about Him, we discover everything real and true about ourselves.

There is another reason we need to hold loosely to personality tests. When God shows us who we are, He shows who He created us to be. That might not look exactly like who we are currently. Life and my circumstances might have developed me into an introverted extrovert or an otter with the head of a lion or a four with a chicken wing or an IMFJ PXQR, you get my drift. But what if God's design for me was something different? Or what if He wants to do a radical life change in an area I think is non-existent? When we walk out the healing, freedom and identity journeys with Him, we discover His master plan for who He created us to be. Free from the limitations that may have been placed on us from the false identities we carried.

When God showed me the picture in my mind of who He made me to be, I no longer felt like that free, joy-filled little girl. He showed me a picture of someone I remembered but did not identify with anymore. Any personality test I took would not have revealed her. Only God could have revealed her and shown me she

> Only God could have revealed her and shown me she was there.

---

66. John 4

was there. Really there. And then take me on the journey to actually being her again.

Please hear my heart. Personality tests are not evil. When I was twenty-four, I took a strengths test and discovered the word *empathy* for the first time in my life. Something that I had always considered a weakness I now saw described as a strength. And now I could see it as a strength in myself and, coupled with the Holy Spirit, see it is an amazing gift I can use for His good. We just need to make sure we do not let these tests become our entire identity. They do not get to override who God says we are or keep us from growing in an area of our lives.

Take me and all my empathy. Part of what empathy means is that I feel everything very deeply. If I am sitting across from you and we are having hot tea (you are more than welcome to have coffee) and you are in the middle of a hard season and feeling lots of strong emotions of sadness and frustration, it means I am feeling those same things as well. I feel what everyone else around me is feeling and everything I am feeling inside. That is a lot of feelings. It is very easy for me to be led by those feelings and to act solely on those feelings because they are so strong and so real. It means in my conversation with you I can become overwhelmed by all you are experiencing and then I might want to draw away from that. Or I may go home and be down and detached for the rest of the day.

But as a Christ follower, I am not just a person who is very high in empathy. That does not define who I am. Did God make me that way? I believe, yes. Even as a very young girl I can remember being upset when others were upset for no reason other than the fact that they were. Crying babies made me cry. I felt all my emotions strongly.

But God has also made me a new creation who received His Holy Spirit. And the fruit of His Spirit brings a lot of great things, including self-control. God also reminds me in scripture that He has given me the spirit of self-discipline.[67]

---

67. 2 Timothy 1:7

This means that while I can use my empathy and emotions for good, I can also use my rational brain and God given self-control to have presence of mind in the middle of all my emotion to still make wise and thoughtful, not just emotional, decisions.

Instead of becoming overwhelmed when I am talking to a friend and they are in the middle of an emotional storm, I can remember the One who calms the storm. I can separate my emotion from the truth of the situation. I don't have to take on this person's feelings and or feel the weight of solving their problems. I can point them to Jesus, invite Him into the conversation and trust Him to be their Savior, not me. When I go home, I choose to remind myself that God is with my friend and comforting her in her time of need.[68] I remember He is good and He has filled my life with good things.[69] My mood lifts and I can have a great evening with my family.

With all my empathy comes a lot of emotions. I feel deeply and can be a bit emotional. Some people (see also: my husband) might even say dramatic. To anyone who knows me, this is no newsflash. Emotions are God given and not bad. But when it comes to all the drama, do I just tell my husband, "This is how I am and how I express myself - get used to it?"

That does not sound like Jesus to me.

With God I do not have to fully reject the things in me like emotion and maybe a little drama. I just need to bring it all into His context and pair it with the other characteristics He says are true about me. It is a beautiful blending of all that I am, framed in the beauty and majesty of the fact that I am made in the image of my Creator. He wants to take every aspect of me, every aspect of my personality, and use it for His good. Use my empathy and emotions to be compassionate towards others. To "rejoice with those that rejoice and mourn with those who mourn".[70]

---

68. Psalm 147:3
69. Psalm 103:5
70. Romans 12:15

At the end of the day it simply means that when I am feeling all the feels and God comes and reminds me about my spirit of self-control, I do not rebuke Him and tell Him I am high in empathy and therefore I cannot be rational and self-controlled. I recognize that His truth overrides all others and if He wants me to grow in an area of weakness I am fully capable of all things because of Him.

Think about someone who would be assessed as an extrovert. Someone who is high energy, loves people and loves chatting up everyone. The life of the party.

That is great. And God can and will use all of those qualities to draw people to Himself. But these passages of Scripture are also true for that talkative extrovert:

"Be quick to listen, slow to speak and slow to become angry."[71]

"Be still and know that I am God." Psalm 46:10

"Jesus often withdrew to lonely places and prayed."[72]

"After the earthquake came a fire, but the Lord was not in the fire. And after the fire there was a the sound of a gentle whisper."[73]

God will want to stretch them in these areas. Teach them about stillness and connecting with God in the quiet places. Remind them to put others first and be quick to listen. Ever heard this verse:

"Do not conform to the pattern of this world, but be transformed by the renewing of your mind. Then you will be able to test and approve what God's will is--his good, pleasing and perfect will."[74]

---

71. James 1:19
72. Luke 5:16
73. 1 Kings 19:12
74. Romans 12:2

What are we to be? Transformed. Changed. God made magnificent creatures when He made us.

We can adapt and change and become more like Christ if we choose to.

If we are new creations, then that means there or no limitations to how we can grow and change in Jesus' name Amen. Every strength is like a two-sided coin. It has a side to it that is a weakness.

Every personality test I will ever take will tell me in some language that I am a planner. I am strategic. It is definitely a strength. I can see around virtual corners to problems that could exist on a certain path. I can think ahead and be prepared. I can plan an event like a boss and I love it all. One of the best days of the year is the day I get my new planner for the upcoming year. Y'all think I am weird, but fellow planners see me. You get me. That is most definitely a strength.

How is that a weakness? I did not know until God showed me. I like order and predictability so much that when the order is not followed and the unplanned presents itself, Sara gets a little panicked. If we have a plan, why would we not follow the plan? I do not understand. I am not a fan of changing the plan. In the past, I would have some very strong emotional responses to the structure and plans not being carried out.

One day a very kind and caring friend asked me a question as we were processing an area where the order and structure was being tested. We addressed what was happening, but then she asked me why I thought I was having such a powerful reaction to the situation. I did not have an answer for her that day. And I did not have an answer for a long time.

It was not until writing this chapter that God made it so abundantly clear. I like order and predictability because it makes me feel safe and in control. Life in my formative years was anything but predictable. Living arrangements changed, stepparents changed, lots of big life things changed often. I could not control any of it, and it made me feel unsafe. When I became old enough to take some of that control back, I took it all. I took it and wrote it down in permanent marker in my planner and felt peace and contentment. When any of that was disrupted, it brought about all the feelings from my childhood of feeling out of control and unsafe.

Once that was revealed, God could address the big fat lies I was believing in all of that. The first was that my safety and peace never actually came from a schedule. My safety and peace come from God. He's the only thing that will never change. He is the only one who will never leave me or forsake me. I draw strength from that, not my gorgeous planner. Predictability is not what keeps me safe. God is.

The other gigantic lie He uncovered was this belief that I ever actually could control or predict anything in my life in the first place! There is no perfect planner that gives me control. A broken clock is correct twice a day, so sometimes I feel like I'm doing it, but I never am. All this revelation did not mean that God wanted me to throw away my planner and never plan another event or make another schedule. I do have strengths in this area. But He wants me to first, invite Him into my planning process. Consult Him on how to use my time. How to plan and coordinate events. He cares about all of it. And second, when the plan gets disrupted and the predictable becomes unpredictable instead of giving in to panic or frustration, He wants me to turn to Him. To remind myself that He is still in control. That I am safe and loved and it is okay to be flexible and go with the flow. To relax and trust that God's got this. He is a way better and more advanced planner than I could ever dream of.

The most important takeaway for us all is God gets the final say. Not some test. We bring those results to Him and process what we learn through the lens of scripture. And when God asks us to grow in a certain area, we don't tell Him we cannot because it is not one of our top five strengths.

So, and in summary, take the test if you want to take the test. It is okay, and Sara never said it was not. Just proceed with caution and hand in hand with the One who knows you best, your loving and intentional Creator.

One Final Word of Caution

Because the enemy likes to come in and try to take anything good and use it for evil, I must give us a last word of caution.

Part of the identity journey is about embracing all of us, even if no one else does. Embracing our quirks, likes, dislikes; being ok with who we truly are. But we do not do that outside of God's instructions to be humble and to think of others as better than ourselves.

The identity journey should never lead us to pride, self-focus, self-centeredness, stubbornness, or having to have our own way.

The point of this entire process - finding freedom, healing and our true identity and purpose - is so we can receive God-given joy. And anything that God gives is meant to be shared and given away. We want to be healed, healthy and whole so that we can be the best versions of ourselves for us but also, and equally important, for others. Being more like Christ means being more focused on others. Using all that we are and all that we have to show Jesus to the world. An attractive, joy-filled life is attractive to the lost. When they see His joy in us, we get an opportunity to tell them about how and why and of course Who.

That is why this whole thing is called a journey. Because we are always moving. This is no time to stop. We do not stop and linger in self-discovery. We do not learn about who we are to use that as a weapon. "This is who I am, deal with it." We embrace who we are and then we turn to embrace others and who they are and help them in their journeys.

We do not all have to like the same things. That is the point. None of this is ever meant to be used as a weapon.

If God is leading our journey, it will lead to peace, humility, and confidence that allows us to love others better, not just ourselves.

The identity journey is one that requires us to discover our false identities and replace them with the truth. It is a process and it takes work, but the joy and freedom that await us make it all worth it.

Change is hard. It is hard for us, and it can also be hard for those that know us. That is okay. Everyone is walking their own journey. And we should let them.

Remember my little fur baby, London? When I got him and I renamed him, I never called him his old name once. He had a new name, London. He belonged to me, and that was the name I gave him.

Anyone who called him Torch would have just proven that they did not know him anymore.

Your Father will never call you a name that He did not give you. And anyone that does is just proving that they don't really know you, not the real you.

Just keep looking to your Father and let Him remind you who you are, again and again, for as long as it takes for the rest of your life.

YOUR IDENTITY JOURNEY

The healing journey and the freedom journey help us let go of the past. They bring us to a place of health and wholeness. Our goal is to live our best life in the present with hope for the future. We are about to shift all our focus to that future, but we have one last step to take first. The last part of the past we have to acknowledge and move on from are our false identities.

1. What are the false names that have been given to you? By yourself or by others?

_____

_____

_____

_____

_____

_____

_____

_____

_____

_____

My guess would be that you identified with some that you read in these chapters. I am sure there are others as well. Take some time to think about and pray about what those might be. Jot down the ones that you are aware of now but know that in the coming days and weeks your eyes might be opened and you might become aware of other false identities you believe in.

We can sometimes find false identities by thinking about how we tell the story of our lives up until this point. What is your story? God has a story, a way that He views you and your life. I do not know exactly what yours is, but I do know what it is not. You are not a victim. In your story from God, you will never be in the victim's role. If you feel like that is your story - abused, rejected, abandoned, cheated on... those are all roles and identities of victims. That is not God's story for your life. Those things may very well have happened to you, but they do not define you. We have to make the choice to stop identifying ourselves as a victim in our story. Let's recognize that false identity and replace it with God's truth.

God most definitely says we are not a victim:

Romans 8:31-39

> *What, then, shall we say in response to these things? If God is for us, who can be against us? He who did not spare his own Son, but gave Him up for us all--how will He not also, along with Him, graciously give us all things? Who will bring any charge against those whom God has chosen? It is God who justifies. Who then is the one who condemns? No one. Christ Jesus who died--more than that, who was raised to life--is at the right hand of God and is also interceding for us. Who shall separate us from the love of Christ? Shall trouble or hardship or persecution or famine or nakedness or danger or sword? As it is written:*
>
>> *"For your sake we face death all day long;*
>> *we are considered as sheep to be slaughtered."*

No, in all these things we are more than conquerors through him who loved us. For I am convinced that neither death nor life, neither angels nor demons, neither the present nor the future, nor any powers, neither height nor depth, nor anything else in all creation, will be able to separate us from the love of God that is in Christ Jesus our Lord.

In this process of realizing false identities, you may find yourself in a place of recalling difficult events from your past. Do not forget all that we have learned in the healing and freedom journeys. You may need to go back through some of the healing process and be sure you have completely forgiven everyone that you need to.

2. As you recognize false identities, the next step is doing the work to replace them with the truth. You do not need to wait to know all the false ones before you speak the true ones. That starts now.

Which of the names we looked at resonate with you the most? Child of God, loved, accepted, friend, worthy, righteous.

_____

_____

_____

_____

Choose a few along with any others that come to mind and jot them down. It is so important to find the scripture that goes with the identity. When the enemy comes whispering the old lies, you will be armed and ready to go with your truth, God's Word that never changes.

Be willing to filter everything back through His Word and accept only truth. No one loves me. False. I am worthless. - False.

Think of it like a game show and you are the host:

"Welcome to today's episode of 'Who Is Sara?'

> Our first contestant, a memory from an old relationship, has given the answer, 'unlovable'. Ok, let's check the Bible to see if the answer is correct. Oh, no. I am sorry that is not correct. The answer we were looking for is lovable. Lovable. We also would have accepted loved by God, God's chosen, God's beloved. But thank you for joining with us today to play 'Who is Sara?'"

See how fun it can be?!

3. What practical things can you do to remind yourself about who God says you are? (Post-it notes on the mirror, a reminder on your phone, scripture memorization...)

_____

_____

_____

_____

_____

_____

_____

_____

_____

4. Where are you with personality tests? Are there any beliefs from those that you are placing above God's truth or equal to it? Are there areas where you have declared you simply are a certain way and maybe God wants to grow or stretch you there? Think of the areas that you would consider your strengths. In what way could that strength also be a weakness? What truth from God's Word can help you overcome those areas?

_____

_____

_____

_____

_____

_____

_____

_____

_____

_____

This is an important place to remind you that this is a journey. A journey is not a quick trip. It is a lifelong process and adventure. Unlearning and relearning takes time. We need to be steadfast and determined but also full of grace for ourselves as we seek to allow God's truth to be our truth. God will not get frustrated with us in our journey. And neither should we be frustrated with ourselves. If you are reading this, you have already done so much. Just keep going!

Plus, it is about to get really good. You were created on purpose for a purpose. The completion of our joy comes when we allow God to show us that purpose and then choose to walk it out with Him. I also have a magic word for you to overcome any doubts about your unique purpose. Yes, a magic word. Come on!

Just a bit further to go.

WHEN THE ROAD GETS ROUGH III: *It's Ok To Laugh*

W hen the road gets rough you have to be alert, awake, and present in your own life to know and see how you are doing. In order to have joy on the rough roads it also helps to have some laughs along the way.

> *"a time to weep and a time to laugh, a time to mourn and a time to dance,"*[75]

It is ok to laugh through the pain, even in a season of death and dying. My family has always handled life with a great sense of humor. We see the lighter side and we enjoy making all the jokes. Maybe even when we shouldn't. My brother and I had lots of great laughs together as we walked out the difficult season with our dad. And Dad was part of most of those. I am so thankful he had his sense of humor for all of his journey. We got to laugh a lot in that season like we had done all of our lives and it helped keep joy in our midst.

Want to hear a secret? I have a recording saved on my computer that is from a podcast of a sports radio talk show I like to listen to. These guys crack me up. One day a few months after my dad had passed away, I was listening to their show, and someone said something, and it came out wrong and they all got so tickled at themselves and they could not stop cracking up. Their laughter was

---

75. Ecclesiastes 3:4

contagious and before I knew it I had cracked a smile and began to laugh. I was laughing so hard, and it was so unexpected. It was the biggest and longest laugh I had experienced since losing my dad. It felt great. I went and downloaded the recording to my computer, and I have listened to it more than a couple of times when I needed a good laugh.

Laughter reminds us we are still alive and capable of feeling something good. Give yourself permission to look for the lighter side of things as you go. Find the things that give you a good, deep belly laugh and repeat as often as necessary.

It is also important to be honest with yourself and your trusted godly relationships about how you are doing along the way.

Here are some great questions to ask yourself on a regular basis: How am I handling all of this? How am I processing? Who am I processing with? Am I taking all of this to God in prayer? And how is all of that working? Am I snapping at strangers? My family? Does it feel like there is a ton of emotion just underneath the surface, just looking for a way out any chance it can get? How are my emotions and feelings?

All of this matters. Our feelings and emotions matter. They need to be felt and experienced and processed, but they do not get to take over and call all the shots. We do not lose our ability to exercise self-control during a very difficult season. My grief is not an excuse to bite everyone's head off that I see in that season. I need to be mature and grown up enough to find a healthy way to process all I am feeling. I do not turn the keys and all control over to my feelings and just strap in like I am along for the ride. I will not be perfect. But that is not the goal. When I do let some of it out and dump it on someone else, I need to be willing to go back and apologize and ask for forgiveness.

Those who know and love us will probably be extending us some much needed and deserved grace and mercy in our difficult season and we need to be grateful and verbalize that as well. But poor strangers that cross our paths, unless you find a gem like Lora, like I did, we cannot take it out on them. We cannot leave a trail of confused, angry people who just got run over by a Mack truck and have no idea why. We are called to more than that, and we are capable of more than that. We will feel all sorts of things, it does not give us permission to sin. "In your anger, do not sin." (Eph 4:26)

Go talk to someone, many someones. A professional Christian counselor, a grief group. Talk as you move through it. Remember, you are still on a journey. We move through our grief and difficult seasons. We do not park and wallow in them. That does not mean we move quickly through it. We may need to go at a snail's pace, but we are moving. Healthy things grow and move. We never compare our process to another's. This is why I highly recommend a reputable Christian counselor. They can help identify if you get stuck and help you keep moving.

Healthy things grow and move.

Stay alert, have some laughs and be aware of how you are doing as you travel the rough road of difficult circumstances.

God has a little more that He would like to show you, but it is the most exciting part of the journey yet. He wants to talk to you about your purpose. Not just any purpose. The purpose He designed specifically for you to do.

THE PURPOSE JOURNEY

A PURPOSE WE CANNOT
LOSE

"They will rebuild the ancient ruins

and restore the places long devastated;

they will renew the ruined cities

that have been devastated for generations. "[76]

D o you remember my friend who passed away from suicide while I was in high school? It was the summer before our junior year. Nothing like that had ever happened in our friend group. He was known and loved by so many. For a bunch of 16-year-olds the loss was painful and confusing, and no one really knew what to do with all of that. We spent lots of evenings together sharing stories and remembering him and crying; a bunch of kids figuring out this grieving thing. One night we were all at an area where we gathered regularly, in an empty field. I do not know if this was just something kids did in the 90's but we had several fields and industrial parking lots we used to gather in.

One of those nights we were talking about our friend, and we all ended up in a circle. It was a pretty intense night of missing him and grieving our collective loss. For reasons I did not understand at the time, and still do not fully understand today, they asked me to pray. I can close my eyes and picture the whole scene; I remember it all

---

76. Isaiah 61:4

so clearly. I had not prayed very much in my life, and I certainly had never prayed in front of a group like that before. I do not know why they asked me. I had gone to church some my sophomore year and there were pockets of us who went to church sometimes, but I certainly did not think of myself as godly or spiritual. But for some reason they asked me and so there I was in a circle of twenty kids or so, all looking at me to pray for our grief-stricken and confused hearts.

What could I do but open my mouth and begin? I will never forget what happened next. As I began to speak, I realized the words were just coming. Coming from somewhere deep inside of me. I was thinking of the things we were feeling and asking God to help us. With an ability and strength I had zero understanding of at the time, I prayed passionately and sincerely for God to comfort us and all who were mourning this loss in that season.

In that moment, even though it would be many years before I was truly walking with God and even though I would go on to make some of the worst decisions of my entire life, in that moment, I believe I tapped into part of the divine purpose that God had placed on my life. And years later, when I did surrender my life completely to God and His calling for my life, that purpose was still intact. I had not forfeited it through poor choices and wrong living. God was always moving, always working. Working behind the scenes. Working on me. Working on my behalf. Nothing was lost. Nothing was wasted. It was all to bring about His good purpose for me.

My purpose was still my purpose, and I could still step into and set my life on the path it was always meant to be on. The path, and journey, with Jesus.

Purpose Defined

The definition of purpose is:

"The reason for which something is done or created or for which something exists."

Purpose was not something I gave any thought to in my life prior to surrendering my life to Jesus.

And even then, it was a slow realization that He created me for a purpose and then still awhile before I could have told you what my unique purpose actually was.

I began to think about and find a sense of purpose while working in full time ministry at my church. For the first time, I began to think that what I was doing was making a difference. I realized that having a purpose felt good and I continued to enjoy discovering the things I was good at and seeing God use those things for His glory.

In case you forgot, I was thirty-five when I met my husband, thirty-six when we got married. I was single for a hot minute. Several, actually. One thing church people like to say is "make your misery your ministry." Meaning, take the thing that is or has been challenging in your life and let God use it to bless you and others.

I am not saying that being single was miserable per se. But it was challenging at times and ultimately it was not what I wanted, so there were hard days and hard seasons.

I chose to let it become my ministry by sharing and speaking openly about being single and following God. I chose to wait for His plan and purpose for me in dating and marriage. The world is pretty vocal about how it thinks we should live our lives. There are lots of ideas out there about dating and how to snag a man. But I had tried the world's way. It left me empty and lonely and broken.

Thankfully, I found healing in God and He went on to make every part of my life make sense. He let the old me fall apart and He put me back together and healed me. All of me. He taught me how to live my whole life submitted to Him. Dating and marriage were obviously very important areas of my life, and it only made sense to me that I would seek Him and His ways for my dating rather than compartmentalize and separate dating from what God had access to. I constantly saw other singles struggling in this area, and I felt inspired to share what God was doing in my journey. Once again, I found purpose.

I really enjoyed it too. I got to lead and be a part of lots of single's bible studies and single's events while on staff at my church. After I left full-time employment there, I started working for myself. I was given opportunities to speak at a few single women and mixed singles events and conferences. I wrote and led a small Bible study for single women and even got to plan and host a single women's retreat! Finding purpose in my season of singleness meant that despite the struggles, it was really a great season of my life. I would have said I was living out my purpose. All the things I was doing felt like things I was created to do. It felt like I was in my sweet spot. I was on the purpose journey and had pretty much arrived. Or so I thought.

Losing My Purpose

Once I got married and was no longer single, I was not sure exactly what I was supposed to do next. I was not sure that having a single women's ministry still made a lot of sense. Adjusting to being a new wife and stepmom of three was an exciting new season of life in and of itself. It changed every part of my life overnight.

Whatever all the reasons were, I paused the singles ministry that had been my primary focus and purpose for so long.

Looking back, I honestly do not know if that was the right decision. One girl on Twitter definitely knew it was not the right decision. I tweeted something about pausing and taking a break from my ministry and she called me out and said "Oh, you snagged a man and now you are done with singles?" Sorry, girl on Twitter. My bad.

Ministry is hard. Doing solo ministry (not on staff at a church or with a non-profit team) was even harder for me. Even now I struggle with consistent motivation, holding myself accountable every day to what I feel called to do. Honestly, at the time I think part of me jumped at the chance to stop and take a break.

Whether it was the right choice or not, God in all His goodness, of course, brought good out of my season of change and taught me a lot.

As I transitioned to wife and stepmom, I started experiencing struggles with feelings of emptiness and purposelessness. It felt like I had lost my identity and the worth and value of my life seemed to slip, at least in my mind. I was not speaking at any events or teaching any Bible studies. I was not sure who I was anymore. I felt I had no purpose. This was all happening right around the same time I realized I was missing joy.

This is where, with God's help, we began to get to work. I thought I had found joy before in living out my purpose doing ministry at my church and for singles. But suddenly without those same opportunities the joy and my purpose were gone. It seemed my joy and sense of purpose was only tied to do the "doing". No doing meant no purpose.

God revealed two big things I was getting wrong about purpose.

He began by addressing what I would have said that my purpose was:

"Being on a stage in front of people sharing God's truth."

That was what I felt filled me up, and therefore that was when I felt joy. And the emphasis for me would have been on the "being on a stage in front of people" part. Just trying to be honest. I love being in front of people. It is fun for me. And so, this is where I felt the most joy as I walked out my purpose.

The first big thing He revealed was that I had some incorrect thinking when it came to purpose. I was struggling with not having any opportunities to be on a stage or be in front of a group to share God's truth. Once I no longer had anything upcoming on the calendar where I was to "go and speak", I felt like I had lost my purpose and my joy.

I had the emphasis in the wrong place. Thankfully, God showed me that my purpose was not found in the first part of that statement:

"Being on a stage in front of people..."

It was found in the last part:

"Sharing God's truth."

God showed me that was a purpose I could live out and find joy in every single day. If being on a stage in front of people is my only purpose, I am in trouble for a few reasons. One reason is that I cannot control other people deciding to have me speak on their stage. And even if I decide to do my own stage and fill a room with people, it is simply not possible to do that every single day. With that formula, I am back on a roller coaster ride with my joy. Up and down.

I realized that purpose was something I needed every day for my joy journey to be complete. I had to reframe what my purpose was and live it seven days a week.

Sharing God's truth is something I can do every day. Even if it is just with myself. But even more than that, I can share God's truth every day with someone through how I love and serve my family; over tea with a friend or a conversation on the phone. Speaking life and love to everyone I come in contact with. This new understanding of my purpose held joy that was abundant and not reserved for conferences or retreats. Redefining purpose in this way was what I needed for the new season I was in and every season in the future.

EVERY DAY PURPOSE

God showed me I could take the smallest part of my day, inject it with His purpose, and change everything. I can live with purpose each and every day. One specific example involved my husband's dry cleaning. (God can and does use every weird, little thing in my life!) When my husband used to travel every week for work, we'd end up with a large drop off for the dry cleaners that I would take every Friday morning.

Later that day or the next day, I would swing by and pick it all up. Once home, I'd take it all to the closet and hang it up for him. Later he would come and undo the twist ties holding it all together, take off all the plastic wrapping and remove the plastic tabs they put under the collars. One day when I was hanging it all up, I felt like God asked me to finish the process completely by removing all the stuff that Paul usually took off. This seemed like a pretty silly request. *Really God? You don't have anything more pressing for me to do than to remove a bunch of plastic from my husband's clothes? Slow day at the office up there?*

Paul never complained about doing it. It only took maybe 60 seconds. Why did I need to worry about it? As teeny tiny and inconsequential as it might seem, I felt like God was challenging me to do this one extra step to show love to my husband. Something he'd never notice or mention, but something that would be nice for him and show him my love and God's love, since it was really His idea to begin with. As crazy as it sounds, it is something I have never forgotten. God also challenged me to pray for Paul while I did it.

167

Pray for his day, his meetings and take a minute to thank God for His provision and for providing for us through my husband the way He did. It opened my eyes to other small gestures I could do throughout my week to show love to Paul. It gave purpose to the otherwise mundane.

God continued to give me more and more tools to live out this purpose and find joy every day. This ended up being a long season of finding purpose, even in not "doing" ministry. At least in the way I would have described it before. Instead, God was teaching me how to live ministry and find purpose in everyday things. I was learning how to be the person He created me to be 24/7, not just for a few hours at a conference one weekend. Not that I was living a double life before, I was not. And not that I could suddenly live a perfect Christian life, I could not. He simply opened my eyes to see Him in every moment. To see opportunities for purpose where I had not seen them before. It does not mean I responded perfectly to every opportunity He showed me, or that I saw all the ones He tried to reveal. But I began to see more and more, and I could embrace more and more of those moments and find purpose in them.

Almost all of those moments of purpose were found at home with me and my hubby and our three kids. There were so many opportunities to share God's truth to be an example to them. I did not always get it right. But I also learned how to own my mistakes, apologize when I got it wrong, and hopefully love them well through it all. Serving our families is one of the best ways to show God's love and live out our daily purpose. Supporting their dreams. Listening to their stories.

Listening to their stories was actually an enormous area where God was growing me. I am very much a morning person. I enjoy getting up before the sun is up. I like my hot tea and my quiet time with the Lord. It is a habit that I established years ago, and I believe life would look very different without it. But because I like early mornings so much it usually means I am asleep by 10:00. Okay sometimes earlier but that is not the point. I am at my best in the mornings. I am fresh and alert. Bright eyed and bushy tailed. Once

8pm hits though, it is a different story. Me and my brain begin winding down about then.

And I have usually had my fill of words for the day. Do you have a word limit for the day? I definitely do. I do not wear a device that counts my steps but something on the inside of me counts the words and when I hit my max, alarms start going off and it's time to shut down.

It gets harder to really engage and make my brain focus. I do not know if you have kids or if all kids are like this, but our three seem to ramp up right about then. Our youngest has usually saved all her words for the last few hours of the day. All of them. This just seems to be the time when conversations get going and stories start flowing.

When I was first on the scene in my new family, it was a big adjustment to all this activity during my winding down in the evening period. There were just so many words. But the Holy Spirit was so, so sweet to me and gave me the gentlest nudge. He encouraged me to not shut them down. And more than that, to engage and to encourage the conversation. Not just pacify. He reminded me it was a blessing that they were sharing, that they were talking and shutting that down could squash it for good. And by His grace, I did not shut it down and I let them flow. It was hard at times. I did not always ask all the questions I could have asked. But I did my best to listen and encourage.

Side note: I am absolutely not saying that if you have disengaged when there are just too many words, there is anything wrong with you. Or that you do not care or have failed as a parent. Do not allow the enemy to come in and speak any of that nonsense over you. This was something specific God was asking *me* to do. Remember, I came into the picture at halftime. My kids were eight, ten and eleven when I showed up. There were thousands of days filled with thousands of words that I was not there for. I missed out on a lot of stories. It gave some added importance to the words I have been here for. And each one of those words helped me get to know them and fall in love with who they are.

It is like how our Heavenly Father is with us. Only He does it perfectly. Always listening, always wanting to hear what is on our heart. What our day was like. What we are excited about, worried about and looking forward to. He wants to know it all. He has no word limit; He can receive all the words and engages us right where we are. Morning or night or middle of the night.

As our kids all became teenagers, it was such a blessing to us how much they shared. They have all always had a great relationship with their dad. They have great talks. And I am so thankful our home was full of their chatter all of those evenings. Now I love to sit and hear them all talking with each other. It makes my heart so happy and so full. That was all part of my purpose journey.

In this season I also found purpose in serving at our church. My husband and I began to serve and lead together. God used that time to refine us as a team. To show us how our strengths could compliment the other. How to share leadership in a marriage. There was some rough going at times, but He was definitely preparing us. I told him recently I believe we are going to write a book together, and he made a joke about me writing and him narrating. God will bring him around. But we couldn't do something like that without these past years of just faithfully serving together. Sometimes we get to use our areas of giftedness, but usually we are just doing what is needed. I was never on staff at our current church, and at one point I would have felt that step was needed in order for what I did there to count as my true purpose. But God blew that lie right up in this season. We found purpose in serving faithfully, leading our teams and supporting the staff however they needed.

Serving my Dad

The next part of my purpose journey was not an easy one. It was in this season that I took on the role of caretaker for my dad, who was battling Parkinson's Disease. Looking back, I can see how God was orchestrating everything. Every little detail of my life aligned, so that I could be there for my dad in the season he needed me. I am so grateful for that. I wasn't working in a physical office full time, and I had great flexibility with the job I did have, working mostly from home.

Finding joy in my purpose in this season with my dad had nothing to do with being on a stage or in front of a group of people. It had everything to do with trusting that I was right where God wanted me to be. And I had the unique and blessed opportunity to show God's love to my dad in a way I would not have been able to otherwise. My dad was always my number one supporter and cheerleader. He loved me unconditionally and did so much for me. I was so grateful for the opportunity to give back to him. And to see him still being the man of God that he always was. I witnessed his kindness and gratitude to all the workers at the facilities he lived in, and the miraculous ways God provided for him to have the care he needed. Parkinson's took what it could from him, but it never got to take his personality, his sense of humor, or his love for God, his family and perfect strangers. It gave us the gift of time. Lots and lots of time together. I am so thankful that God made it part of my purpose to walk that journey with the father I was so thankful for.

My dad got to live out his purpose in that season as well. It was hard, for sure and he struggled. But he still loved, and he loved well. I got to see evidence of that just recently. My nephew is eight years old. He was not even two when Paul and I met. For as long as Jaxon can remember, I have been in his life. He knows me well, and he knew my dad. Granddad Ken. My dad loved Jaxon. The whole time Jaxon knew my dad, he was battling Parkinson's. Eventually my dad was in a wheelchair and unable to walk, but we still did family dinners and celebrated birthdays and holidays together. My dad was in Jaxon's life for a relatively brief season, but it was meaningful all the same. My sister-in-law told me recently that as they were putting up their Christmas tree last year, Jaxon paused when putting up an ornament, something about the ornament or the activity reminded him of my dad, and he said he missed Grandad Ken. That is amazing to me. He does not just remember a man who was sick and in a wheelchair.

Because my dad lived out purpose in his hardest season, Jaxon remembers a man who saw him and loved him. A man who listened to his stories and asked how he was doing. My dad had purpose in that season, and he fulfilled it. I had purpose in that season. And I am so thankful I could fulfill it.

Though there were no stages, no teaching, and no audiences, it was a purpose-defining season. Along my purpose journey, I learned that I have purpose every single day, regardless of what I am doing or not doing.

Identifying our daily purpose and living that out are so incredibly important to the journey to joy. Our lives matter. What we do every day matters.

God showed me my thinking about my purpose was wrong because I was only looking for "big" opportunities to live out purpose on a large scale. He showed me I have countless big opportunities to live on purpose every day and that is the key to really living out the purpose journey with Him. I have a daily purpose.

BIG PICTURE PURPOSE

The second thing God showed me about purpose was that we do not have just one. We have daily purpose, and we also have, for lack of a better term, big picture purpose. We are called to love and serve our families and friends well each day. We are also called to use our unique strengths and abilities to do specific things in the way that only we can do them. Leave our mark, our unique fingerprint in the time we are on this earth. Our big picture purpose is to have a Kingdom impact on the world around us.

Before you close this book and say you do not have a big picture purpose on that large of a scale for your life, let me show you what I mean.

You caught a bit of this story in my journal entries in *When the Road Gets Rough II*. There was a lot going on in the weeks before my dad passed away. We were trying to get him accepted into a temporary rehabilitation facility to regain some strength and mobility he had lost while being sick for a week. We were also looking at a new living facility to move him to that had an extra level of care that he was needing. Lots of moving parts. At the same time life was going on and I had a regular doctor's appointment and was paying bills and ended up on the phone with someone in the billing department of my doctor's office. There was a charge on my account for a procedure I had not done. I called to have it fixed and she said the doctor made a note that I had requested it and she had done it. I snapped. I proceeded to, very loudly, tell her that was not at all the case, and I was not paying for it and on and on. Not even close to my finest moment.

As soon as I finished, I regretted it all. I took a deep breath and apologized. I could barely get my apology out and this sweet woman, her name was Lora, asked me what was going on. Was I ok and was there anything she could do? Somehow, she knew I was at a breaking point. Well, that was all it took, and I proceeded to tell her, through my sobs, everything that was going on and why I was so stressed. She stopped everything and started asking me about my dad. She asked me how he was, and she asked me to share with her one of my favorite things about him. *What? Who was this amazing woman?!* We had the most peaceful conversation and at the end she encouraged me to reach out to "my people" for some support and love. I did too. As soon as we hung up, I reached out to my counselor as well as my group of girlfriends and we scheduled a girl's dinner for what would end up being the evening of the day my dad died. All because of Lora and how she chose to have an impact on me that day.

She even checked on me a few weeks later and was incredibly kind and compassionate when she learned my dad had passed. Not surprisingly, I did find out she is a Christian. A Christian living out her purpose in her chosen profession and making a Kingdom impact on the world around her, namely me.

That is big picture purpose and we all have it.

For me this was the ministry calling that I first started discovering in my late twenties. This was the part I had loved. The part I was the most excited about. I always wanted to speak and teach and write.

But now, being on the purpose journey and being in a position to step into all of the big picture purpose, I found myself hesitating. Unsure about how to proceed but the real truth was I was afraid of proceeding at all.

Roadblocks

There are going to be roadblocks trying to keep us from stepping into our big picture purpose. We will all have them. We just have to identify what they are and work our way through them with the Lord. He will always provide a way.

The primary reasons I was afraid to step into my big picture purpose are pretty common.

Fear and Insecurity

I am super blessed with amazing women friends. A few of them are in similar lanes that I am in when it comes to our callings. We have some very similar strengths. I know some very gifted writers and speakers. They do amazing things. Apart from them, there are also a *few* women out there, whose names you know, in the world who are crazy talented writers and speakers. They have amazing ministries and help thousands of people every year. They write inspiring books and host conferences and share God's Word in life-changing ways.

I do not know if you can see where I am going with this or not. But it could cause someone (me) to question whether there is even any point in getting out of bed in the morning.

Why on earth do I think the world needs another Christian writer or speaker? Do we really need another devotional?! It is easy for me to think all those women already have it pretty well covered. So, I am just going to go eat some dairy-free ice cream and watch *Law and Order.*

When you discover your unique, big picture purposes, there is a pretty good chance you will know or know of someone who is already having success in that field. Do not let the enemy use that to lie to you and tell you, you are not needed.

There have been times I have doubted whether the world really needed me and my specific and unique purpose. One word changed my thinking. Just one simple word. It's a magic word and it will work for you too.

Ready?

Jelly.

That's not a typo.

Jelly. But not just jelly. Jam, preserves, marmalade, conserves, chutney, fruit butter, curds, single fruit, mixed fruit, strawberry, blueberry, apple, blackberry, plum, red, raspberry, peach, apricot, triple berry, rhubarb, gooseberry, current, cranberry, elderberry, boysenberry, sweet orange, peach, mango, cherry, pineapple, jalapeño! Then you have all-natural all those, added sugar all of those, low sugar all of those, sugar-free all those, organic all of those. Some have fruit and honey. Now some have jelly and peanut butter together. Some have seeds and some are seedless. Whew.

Y'all! It is mashed up fruit! We are talking about mashed up fruit and yet the next time you are in the grocery store head over to the jelly aisle and you are going to be overwhelmed at all the options of mashed up fruit. There is so much jelly! And this is not a new thing. There has been a lot of jelly for a very long time. If our world can sustain all these different kinds of mashed up fruit, then I think we can handle some more speakers and some more teachers and some more coaches and some more nurses and some more doctors and everything else you can think of!

Just today over 300,000 babies were born. They all need mentors and parents and accountants and authors. They need to read books that have not been written and cook recipes that have not been created yet.

The truth is, the world needs my specific flavor, and it needs yours too. You cannot be the exact flavor that I am, and I cannot be yours. We might both be strawberry preserves, but I am sugar-free with seeds and you are low sugar without seeds. God called us to be those exact flavors.

When the enemy comes and tries to tell us we cannot be called to do something because so and so already does it, we remind him and ourselves about the jelly. We cannot let ourselves get intimidated by seeing other people in their giftedness. That is when we celebrate them! We realize she is a very amazing apple fruit butter, and I cannot be that apple fruit butter but I'm going to go be my sugar-free, strawberry preserves with seeds.

The bottom line is if I do not step into who I am supposed to be, there's going to be a hole on the shelf. I absolutely believe this is true. I can forget for a second or two at times. That's why I have an actual picture of the jelly aisle from my local grocery store blown up and framed in my office. Anytime my confidence falters or I see a friend or amazing woman do something outstanding and wonder if I can cut the mustard (might as well keep going with the food analogies) I just look at my jelly picture and realize one of those jars is me and I have a place on the shelf.

We all do. Without every one of us there would be a very obvious hole in a very specific place in the world.

A hole in the life of someone we are supposed to love and shape and mold. A hole in an area of discovery that we are supposed to advance.

Words missing that are supposed to be read or spoken to inspire and teach.

A new product or business that will not ever exist.

A team that will not be led or developed how it could. and the list goes on.

We are unique. We have strengths. We have purpose. We are jelly.

Long-Suffering

As God led me into big picture purpose it was so exciting! Speak – yay! Teach – yay! Write – yay! A book – nooooooo.

I was excited to do it all, but the absolute truth is, I never wanted to write a book. And I told God as much. And I was very specific as to why and my why really had to do with the way I thought He made me.

It ties into another roadblock that was threatening my big picture purpose and it is kind of embarrassing to admit.

Here are a few details about Sara. I am a great starter. I really like starting things. And I actually really like finishing things too. I love lists. And what is the best part of a list? (All together:) When you cross something off! Something is done. Yay! So, in summary, I enjoy starting and I enjoy finishing.

What I really like is for those two things to be close together. The in between, actual doing part is the hardest part for me. I like that part to be as short as possible. Especially if it is difficult for me. Therefore, I enjoy writing blog posts and devotionals. Short and sweet. Even if it is tough, I can manage. Short suffering, I can do. Long suffering, not so much my thing. Unfortunately for me:

> *But the fruit of the Spirit is love, joy, peace, long suffering, kindness, goodness, faithfulness, gentleness, and self-control.*[77]

Ugh. LONG suffering. Why does it have to be long?

I knew that writing a book would be one of those long-suffering exercises. I knew I wanted no part of it. *Give me all the short suffering Lord! I will take it all. Just please leave the long suffering to someone else!*

I was never interested in the idea of writing a book. At. All. And then suddenly I found myself in the midst of feeling called to write a book. What was I thinking?!

And y'all, it was hard. There were most definitely seasons when I thought it would not happen. I doubted whether I really was going to be able to finish. And to be honest, I was kind of ok with that. I thought I could just leave it alone and move on and live my life. I ran into one big problem, though. I wasn't able to do anything else that I wanted to do.

---

77. Galatians 5:22

During the journey of writing this book, I kept having ideas. I always have ideas. Things I wanted to do. Inspiration! Podcasts. Retreats. But it was all fruitless. Every time I began to go down one of those roads, I either ran out of steam and inspiration, or I hit walls and obstacles that I could not overcome. And each time I felt God speak to me. Each time I gently felt Him remind me about the last thing He had asked me to do. I had to write, and I had to finish.

I think part of the reason I had to finish was simply to prove to myself that I could. He was trying to show me I was not a quitter. I could do hard things. And now that I am nearing the finish line, I can see. I can see that all the other things I have been dreaming about along the way, they are all coming. I just had to do this first. It overwhelms me to say I did not quit. I can look ahead to anything else coming on my purpose journey, and I have confidence that I'll be able to do it. I can do hard things.

Work

Another roadblock that causes us to avoid stepping into big picture purpose is we are not sure what is going to be required of us. Or maybe we have an inkling of what will be required, and we do not like the idea of it.

I did that. I knew some of what writing a book was going to require of me and I was not sure I could do it or that I wanted to do it.

There are some things, for all of us, that living out big picture purpose will require, but they are not things to be feared or avoided. We do not like the unknown, so it is best to just get these out in the open right now.

Living out our unique, big picture purpose will require:
Work.

Ouch. Is that a four-letter word or what? Work gets a bad rap. It is what we do to live. To survive.

To pay the bills. But God did not give us work as a punishment. Work is the opposite of bad. (See also: work is good) Our God is a god of work. He worked to create the world we love. He worked to create man. And then He did some resting. But do you know why the resting is so good? Because of work!

Listen, I love Christmastime a lot. But I will be the first to admit it would not be special if every day really was Christmas. There is a reason God created change in our world. The sun rising and setting; the seasons changing. We appreciate many things because of the way we experience them. Whether or not we want to admit it, days of rest on end would not fulfill us. Boredom would set in, and the God-given desire in us to do something would rise up. In eternity we will not be lounging around all day sipping drinks with umbrellas in coconuts.

We were created for work. It feels good and it connects us to our Creator, the ultimate worker.

Genesis 1 tells us, "In the beginning God created..."

He created all we see. That took a lot of work. He also created man. He created man and asked him to be fruitful and to look over all that God had created. He asked him to work:

"The Lord God took the man and put him in the Garden of Eden to work it and take care of it."[78]

And before anyone tries to say that work came because of sin, let me clarify that all of this took place before sin had entered the picture. Before the woman had even been created. Work is not a punishment.

Work is good. God created us for work. We have a part to play, things to do. It is not a bad thing, it is by design.

Noah built.

Abraham led.

David fought.

Mary carried, delivered and raised a son.

---

78. Genesis 2:15

God did His part in all of their lives, and they did theirs. They all did the work.

The truth about our God-given purpose is that at the core it all boils down to the same thing - serving others. However the "doing" actually manifests itself, if it is God-given, it will always result in serving the good of others. From medicine, to teaching, to parenting, pastoring, business and finances - God will use us in every area that exists to serve someone else.

It only makes sense that the enemy would try to keep us from all of that by making us want to avoid what it will take:

Selflessness

The idea of having to serve other people and put them before ourselves. Double ouch. We really do not like the idea of it not being about us. Again though, we were created, hard-wired to enjoy serving others.

> *"Do nothing out of selfish ambition or vain conceit. Rather, in humility value others above yourselves, not looking to your own interests but each of you to the interests of the others."*[79]

The thing about selflessness though is it can really be the key to keeping us on track and in the game. If my purpose is just all about me, if I am writing this book just for myself but on this particular day myself is not so interested in writing then it is really easy for me to spend my time doing other things. I am the only one affected, so why does it matter? I got stuck in this trap more than a few times in the endeavor of writing this book.

But if I am choosing to operate out of selflessness, then the reason I am writing this book is not me, it is YOU. I am writing this book for you. I believe that the things God has taught me and used

---

79. Philippians 2:3-4

to change my life could really, truly literally benefit you. Like, for real. I believe God can use this book to bring more joy into your life through healing and freedom. To give you identity and purpose. If I do not particularly feel like writing, I can acknowledge that but then I remind myself of my purpose and my "why" behind all of this. And guess what? You then inspire me to continue. You have helped me write this book. You have helped me to not quit - thank you! That only comes when I choose to believe it is not about me and I choose to make it about you.

Additionally, many secular studies note that volunteering (serving others) is tied to reduced stress, anxiety and depression. The times over the last few years when I was avoiding my purpose were some of the hardest and lowest. I would become so focused on my own life, my junk and funk, and it would become all-consuming. But when I stepped into my purpose and let it be about the good of others, it took my focus off me and put it onto others, put it onto you actually. The truth is, I might not do this just for me, but I can and will do it for you.

If we do not embrace the selflessness God has called us to, it could keep us from living out the purpose He has for us.

The third thing living out our big picture purpose requires will be the key to numbers one and two. On my own I cannot do the work and I cannot be the selfless person I need to be to walk out my purpose the way God intended.

Connection to The Source

"I can do everything through Christ who gives me strength."[80]

"With man this is impossible, but with God all things are possible."[81]

---

80. Philippians 4:13
81. Matthew 19:26

"I am the vine; you are the branches. If you remain in me and I in you, you will bear much fruit; apart from me you can do nothing"[82]

Do you see the picture being painted here? God is clearly telling us we need Him. We need Him in order to make it through every day. We need Him to experience joy. We absolutely need Him to walk in and fulfill our God-given purpose. Look at Jesus:

"But Jesus often withdrew to lonely places and prayed..."[83]

Jesus gave them this answer: "Very truly I tell you, the Son can do nothing by himself; he can do only what he sees his Father doing, because whatever the Father does the Son also does.[84]

Okay, let's make this as simple as possible. Jesus was fully God. He was capable of wondrous miracles. He was present at the creation of the Earth. And yet, when He came

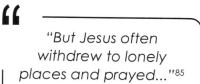

"But Jesus often withdrew to lonely places and prayed..."[85]

back to that same Earth, He did not walk out His calling alone. The very opposite. He did it walking in step with God the Father.

If God the Son needed God the Father to walk out His purpose here on Earth, how much more do you and I need Him?

We simply cannot do this alone.

Now technically we can. At least for a little while. I have done it. One of my favorite moves is getting out in front of God. Classic Sara. I have long legs so if I am not careful, I end up outpacing God and realize I am on my own agenda. I get excited when He gives me an idea or puts a vision on my heart. But He is not giving me those

---

82. John 15:5
83. Luke 5:16
84. John 5:19

things so that I can run out on my own to attempt them. He is giving me those things so that we can walk them out together.

When I do get out ahead of Him, it never ends well. I can tell pretty quickly when I have done it by the desert, desolate surroundings. I feel very alone and it seems nobody else is nearby. And nothing I do seems to produce much fruit. I might be excited and full of what I think is motivation and inspiration, but like a tire with a big gash in it, I quickly start to deflate.

That is when I know. I have jumped ahead. I went too fast. I am not connected to The Source and this is all coming from my own strength, and my own strength is failing.

The other way I know is that because it is coming from my strength, I get weary. I get frustrated.

And soon I am unsure about where I am and what the next step is.

That is when I realize that the next step is to take a step back. Back to the Lord. Back to walking in step with Him. Back to trusting His timing and His plan. Back to realizing that the greatest purpose anyone has ever had was the purpose of being Savior for the world. And The One who carried that purpose never seemed to be in a rush. He was never harried or hurried. He made His time alone with God a priority. He had time for everyone He encountered because He realized it was all tied together when He was tied to the Lord.

> **He realized it was all together when He was tied to the Lord.**

If Romans 8:28 is true and:

"God works all things for the good of those who love him and are called according to his purpose."

Then I can trust that when I am walking with God, everything I encounter is going to be used for my good.

I know it is easier said than done. Believe me. I am a strategic planner. The day I get my planner every year is a mini-Christmas for me. I know, I have said that already, but it is so true. I love making a good plan. But God can plan circles around me.

One of the biggest parts of planning something big is walking through the event in your mind ahead of time. This is the best way to catch things you might have missed and become aware of potential obstacles. Even my best strategic planning session cannot catch everything. I can imagine something in the future, but I am not actually seeing the future. Sadly, I cannot do that, but God can. He is already in the future, and He knows all that is waiting around the corner. So why on earth wouldn't I involve Him in every part of my planning?

God is the one who has given us our purpose and called us to it. He has equipped us, and He will help us see it through. But we must stay connected to Him.

When I am connected to The Source I am now fully equipped to do the work and to be selfless. I am equipped to make a Kingdom impact, I am ready for my purpose journey.

THE POWER OF BELIEF

I strongly believe that we cannot live a joy-filled and content life without seeking and acknowledging that we have purpose. Each one of our days has purpose. Our lives have purpose.

It is common sense if you think about it. If I do not know or believe that there is any reason or point to my existence today, how is that belief going to manifest itself? What will be the point to even getting out of bed? As a depression survivor, I strongly believe that the enemy tries to steer us down the path towards depression in many ways. But one sure-fire way is by taking away or making us believe we don't have any purpose.

When I live without purpose, it impacts every area of my life. I avoided stepping fully into my purpose for so long. Now that I am walking it out, I can't imagine stopping. It has made everything better.

There is absolutely a reason that we exist. Why we woke up today. Our lives have meaning. Tremendous, divine meaning. When we partner with God, we get the chance to walk that out every day.

More than that, He will always equip us to fulfill the purposes He has for us. He does not give us something to do and then leave us on our own to complete it. He walks with us every step of the way. He is our encourager and our coach. Our counselor. And the greatest thing ever is He never gives up on us. Even when we give up on ourselves. Do you have any idea how many times I have "quit" writing this book? Oh, my gosh! Countless. But I kept coming back, and God is so incredibly good and faithful. He meets me right back here every time. He leads me, inspires me, and encourages me to get back up again and keep going. My first thoughts for this book came over four years ago! I have certainly had enough hours to write a collection of books in that amount of time. But that's not my story. I've danced around my purpose, grabbed ahold of it tightly, put in on the back shelf, moved it to a box in the attic and picked it up and dusted it off and reclaimed it so many times I have lost count. My purpose never expired while I wavered. God never gave up. Thankfully, that is not in His nature.

> *"If we are unfaithful, he remains faithful, for he cannot deny who he is."*[85]

God is faithful, so I will continue to get up again and come back to Him and come back to the purpose He has for me. I will not quit. I will not stop. With Him, I have learned that I am capable of walking into all He has for me on this purpose journey.

He is inviting you to do the same. Your life has meaning. Your life matters. You have purpose every day and you have big picture purpose as well. There is no pressure with owning our purpose. It is the opposite. When we embrace our purpose every day, we will be filled with motivation and inspiration and joy. We will realize we are walking step by step with a Father who created us and designed us to take these very steps with Him.

The goal of the healing, freedom and identity journeys was to get us here. To our God -given purpose. When we walk that out with the Lord, everlasting joy will be ours. But do not just take my word for it, experience it yourself.

---

85. 2 Timothy 2:13 NLT

YOUR PURPOSE JOURNEY

Part of your joy journey is discovering with God the purposes He created you for. He has a daily purpose for you each day and big picture purpose as well.

Discovering big picture purpose doesn't mean you then have to quit your job and do what you feel created to do 24/7. You may not even want to. But you can find and step into the things God created you to do and add more of that purpose into your life. Maybe one day you will decide you do want to quit your job and do those things. If that is or becomes your desire, I believe God will get you there!

All purpose matters.

Laundry does not make me feel fulfilled. I do not hate it, I kind of like it, but I do not feel like I am fulfilling my God given destiny every time I fold my husband's underwear. Yet I do it every week. I do not really love cooking. But we have to eat, and currently my husband works full time and is in meetings or on calls most of the week. We both work from home but I have more time and flexibility to take care of those things around the house, so I do. The truth is he does a lot even with all his meetings and calls.

The chores around the house are not the things that get me excited, but they still need to get done.

We are all going to have a list of things we do that are not part of our creative make up. We can still do them with joy, though. The key is finding and keeping our gratitude and kingdom perspective and recognize we can still have purpose in them.

Jesus had a big picture purpose: be Savior for the world by dying on the cross. It was a big thing, on a big stage, but did He have purpose every day until then? Of course, He did. So can we.

Before you begin, don't forget: God announced His love and approval for Jesus before He ever did any miracles.[86]

The same is true for us. God is already pleased with you. That is not why we discover and live out our purpose. You already know your identity in Him, now you get to walk it out with Him.

The reason purpose is so important is none of us were created by accident. Regardless of the familial circumstances we entered into, the decision for us to exist was God's alone. He decided. He decided I should exist, and He decided you should exist. God is intentional with His creation. There is purpose behind everything that He does and because of that it means you and I have purpose too. There is a purpose to our lives, a reason we exist. We are not destined to simply take up space for a hundred years. We are also not solely created so we can spend eternity in heaven. Of course, that is the first proper step towards walking in our purpose, accepting Jesus as our Savior and changing our eternity. But that is not where our purpose ends. If it did, we would all go to heaven the instant we accepted Christ.

"For we are God's handiwork, created in Christ Jesus to do good works, which God prepared in advance for us to do."[87]

Believing we have no purpose is really no option. If I have no purpose, my life does not matter, then what I do with my time certainly does not matter. If I spend hours a day scrolling on my phone, who cares? There is not a greater purpose for my time, so what I do does not matter. On the days we mindlessly stumble along, unaware of Him or His purpose for the day, the time drags on; we feel down and disconnected; we feel scattered and at the end of the day there is nothing but empty hours that have passed and the realization we have

---

86. Matthew 3:17
87. Ephesians 2:10

to do it all again the next day. That is no way to live. That is not living on purpose, and that is not living with joy.

You do not want to live a life where you believe there is no reason for your existence. That is not a good place to be. It gets very dark and very lonely very quickly. And ultimately you end up not caring if you exist at all. Frankly, I believe that is the devil's ultimate plan. He wants to take us out and make us ineffective one way or another. He can distract us all our lives or he can actually get us believing we have no purpose. I know without a shadow of a doubt that you absolutely, positively, 100% have God-given purpose. Your life has great value and meaning.

Remember the definition of purpose:

"The reason for which something is done or created or for which something exists."

There is a reason that you were created and a reason that you exist. Your entire life has a purpose.

God has plans for your life - good plans! And He wants to do things with you and through you. The number of possibilities is endless! But there is a purpose for your life. It is not just a big picture purpose either. A big picture consists of small individual strokes. Each day has purpose. Each day matters.

I want to make sure you are aware of one more thing before we continue. Have your ever thought about why God used people the way He did in Scripture?

Take Moses for example. You can read his story in the book of Exodus. One of the things Moses is most known for is being used by God to free the people of Israel from Egyptian slavery. God used him to speak to Pharoah, the Egyptian leader, and - to set a record for making a really long story, really short - Pharoah eventually let the Israelites go.

I wondered one time about why God chose to use Moses that way? Why He chooses to use any of us for that matter? He is God.

He can do anything at any time. He spoke to Moses in a burning bush. He could have picked up that bush and dropped it in front of Pharoah and told him directly to let the Israelites go.

But He didn't. He chose instead to speak to Moses and work with him. Not because He had to but because He *wanted* to. God wants to use us. He wants to work with us. He wants to write books with us and practice medicine with us and raise our kids with us and grocery shop with us and do every other little or big thing *with* us. *With* you.

He created you on purpose, for a purpose and now wants to walk out that purpose with you every day. Will you let Him?

Let's start with our daily purpose. Here is a non-exhaustive list of things we are called to as Christ-followers:

A. Share the gospel
B. Serve one another
C. Love one another

1. What does living out that daily purpose in your life look like?

_____

_____

_____

_____

_____

_____

_____

_____

_____

_____

2. Who are you called to love and serve? How can you find purpose as you love and serve them?

_____

_____

_____

_____

_____

_____

_____

_____

_____

_____

3. Where and how can you share the gospel?

_____

_____

_____

_____

_____

_____

_____

_____

_____

_____

4. How can you make this purpose part of your life and remind yourself about it when you forget or get off track?

_____

_____

_____

_____

_____

_____

_____

_____

How about the big picture purpose God put YOU on this planet for:

5. First of all, how does that statement sit with you? Do you believe you have a unique, big picture purpose? Why or why not?

_____

_____

_____

_____

_____

_____

_____

_____

6. Especially if your answer is no, take some time and prayerfully ask God about it. Jot down anything He speaks to you.

_____

_____

_____

_____

_____

_____

_____

_____

_____

A great tool for finding your unique giftedness is the people around you. Trusted people. Remember when we discussed trusted people? These people love and follow Jesus. They pray for you and are for you.

They do not tear you down. They may, and should, offer constructive correction from time to time, but even then, they support and encourage you.

Schedule a tea (or coffee) date with one of them. Ask them to pray about the strengths and unique gifts that they see in you and come prepared to share that with you. That might feel like a big, scary ask, but it will be worth it. Walking out our purpose can be risky, but the ultimate reward is always worth it.

We have established or are establishing that you were created for unique, big picture purpose.

7. Do you know what some of those things might be? It is ok if you do not know for sure but take a guess. What things have always

come naturally to you? What do you love to do? Are there things that you do and people wonder at how you do it and to you it just seems to be part of who you are? Is there an ongoing theme to your conversations with God and the areas He is revealing things to you?

In the famous movie, *Chariots of Fire*, the main character, Eric Liddell is a runner. In the movie he is trying to describe to his sister how it feels for him to run.

"I believe God made me for a purpose, but he also made me fast. And when I run, I feel his pleasure."

Are there things that when you do them, you feel God's pleasure? You can feel that you were created to do that thing?

It is also beneficial to look at the things that might be tough for you, but they seem to always be coming up in your life. For me, speaking in front of people is easy and something I enjoy. I get to exercise that unique gifting and purpose. However, as you are currently reading the words I wrote, I also believe part of my unique calling and giftedness is for writing. I can say I believe that now, but it took time for me to accept that was part of my purpose. From the very beginning of our relationship and marriage, my husband has been encouraging me to write. He always felt that was a part of my purpose. Others that know me have spoken the same thing over me. Eventually I began to see they were right, and I agreed with them, and God, that writing would be part of my purpose story.

That does not mean it comes easily for me. It is more difficult and takes more time and thought than preaching a message does for me. The simple truth is I feel so comfortable up on a stage it can be easy for me to do that in my own strength. But writing? Not so much. I feel much more dependent on God for this process. Do not get me wrong, I do not step on a stage where I am sharing God's truth without Him. He is involved in the process, and I do not do that on my own. But the actual strength to do it is already within me. I believe, placed by Him, but it is just there. From the time I was a little child, I enjoyed the spotlight. Whether through dance or theater, I didn't fear being in front of people.

Writing is more of a discipline. It is fun at times. Once I get going, it is an enjoyable process. But it is a very long process. Many times, it is just plain commitment and self-discipline to sit down and ask God what He wants me to write. The process of beginning this book was so difficult for me. I sat and cried in front of my computer so many times because I did not know what I was supposed to write, I just knew I was supposed to write something. I learned later that the point of that season was not what I wasn't writing. It was not about the what. It was about the Who. I sat down every day and I cried out to Him. I waited on Him. I was completely dependent on His guidance and direction. God wants to use us in areas where we will be dependent on Him just like that.

God will use areas where He has given us natural talents and abilities. He also wants to use areas where He can stretch us. I do not believe this means that we can truly be anything that we want, though. Sorry. If you are 4'8" and you want to be MVP of the WNBA, I do not know if that is the purpose God has called you to.

Before you potentially head too far down the wrong path, let me give you an example of how this could play out. Do you know those scenes in movies where people faint at the sight of blood? I have never done that, but I have had to sit down out of fear that I might. And not just at the sight of blood, but at the very mention of some gruesome injury. One time I was in a medical clinic and a woman was having her blood drawn down the hall. Suddenly she let out a bit of a yelp from the back room. Y'all, I almost hit the floor. Thankfully, there was a chair nearby where I was able to sit down. Just knowing she was back there and stuff with blood was happening and seemingly not happening well almost made me pass out.

Seriously. When it happens I get a funny sensation in my stomach, almost like a drop on a roller coaster, and I have to sit down. I can't watch super gory stuff on TV or movies either.

Here is the thing though, I love helping people. I do not like to see people hurt and I would love to be able to make them "all better".

What if I got it in my head that I want to help people so I should become a doctor or a nurse? God created me to help people, and this is a way to help people, so that is what I want to do. Okay, but how much help am I really going to be passed out cold on the floor?

There is an element of wisdom and common sense when it comes to looking at our unique giftedness. I am not saying, Sara is not saying, that God never wants to do the impossible and do something miraculous in the life of someone by having them succeed in an area where they have no earthly ability. But I am saying that in those instances I believe God will make it absolutely, abundantly clear. Like burning bush clarity people.

Outside of that, I think we are best sticking to areas we see Him inviting us into. With a willingness to be asked to walk on water from time to time.

8. So, now that we have established all of that - what do you feel called to do? Why do you think God placed you on this earth, at this time, in this place?

_____

_____

_____

_____

_____

_____

_____

_____

_____

_____

9. If you are not already, how can you begin to walk in purpose with Him?

_____

_____

_____

_____

_____

_____

_____

_____

_____

_____

10. If you already are, how can you continue and/or are there some other areas He is inviting you into? Places to take a step of faith?

_____

_____

_____

_____

_____

_____

_____

_____

_____

_____

11. What are potential or existing roadblocks in your way?

_____

_____

_____

_____

_____

_____

_____

_____

_____

12. Are there things God wants to help you move through with Him? Or are they "fainting at the sight of blood" type indicators that maybe your purpose lies in another direction?

_____

_____

_____

_____

_____

_____

_____

_____

_____

_____

When you start to figure out your purpose and unique calling, the enemy will come in and start to give you reasons not to step into it. One of the ways he does that is by bringing up other people that are already doing what you are called to do. And he will even tell you they are doing it better. This is when you remind him and yourself about all the jelly.

The truth is, we can learn from the amazing people out there that are already doing well what we feel called to do. We do not let fear or intimidation keep us from celebrating them, cheering them on, praying for them and letting God teach us through what they are already doing. Embrace them. There is community for you there. You may run into some who do not embrace that same thinking and that is okay. Keep going and find the ones that do. So many people out there feel called to help those that are coming along in their field. Find them and learn. And then turn around and see who is behind you, just getting started, and choose to be a teacher to them.

The absolute best thing you can do is take a step.

Be willing to take a step in the "wrong" direction if the alternative is not taking a step at all. I put wrong in quotation marks because if your heart is for the Lord and your goal is to walk out your purpose with Him then there are no wrong steps. Remember: He works it all out for our good, anyway. Take a step and trust Him to redirect as needed. It is much easier to steer a moving ship.

Do not ever forget. You are jelly. You are unique. There is a place on the shelf only for you.

WHEN THE ROAD GETS ROUGH IV: *Grief + Purpose = Joy*

L ook how far we have come! Go ahead, take a peek at the path you have traversed. We have been on a healing journey, a journey to freedom and finally, the journey to find our true identity and purpose in Jesus.

If you have also been on the rough road of life during our journey, I have one more piece for you as well. It is the best piece of all because it is Jesus. We know that the life of Jesus was not an easy one. He endured much we will never be able to relate to. While we cannot relate to all He experienced, He can most definitely relate to all we walk through. I specifically want to show you His response after the experience of losing His friend, and His cousin, John.

Jesus after John the Baptist was killed -

In Matthew 14:10-23:

> *So John was beheaded in the prison, and his head was brought on a tray and given to the girl, who took it to her mother. Later, John's disciples came for his body and buried it. Then they went and told Jesus what had happened.*

> *As soon as Jesus heard the news, he left in a boat to a remote area to be alone. But the crowds heard where he was headed and*

followed on foot from many towns. Jesus saw the huge crowd as he stepped from the boat, and he had compassion on them and healed their sick.

That evening the disciples came to him and said, "This is a remote place, and it's already getting late. Send the crowds away so they can go to the villages and buy food for themselves."

But Jesus said, "That isn't necessary—you feed them."

"But we have only five loaves of bread and two fish!" they answered.

"Bring them here," he said. Then he told the people to sit down on the grass. Jesus took the five loaves and two fish, looked up toward heaven, and blessed them. Then, breaking the loaves into pieces, he gave the bread to the disciples, who distributed it to the people. They all ate as much as they wanted, and afterward, the disciples picked up twelve baskets of leftovers. About 5,000 men were fed that day, in addition to all the women and children!

Immediately after this, Jesus insisted that his disciples get back into the boat and cross to the other side of the lake, while he sent the people home. After sending them home, he went up into the hills by himself to pray. Night fell while he was there alone.

This story is such a gift. Jesus, through His example, gives us keys for exactly how to process our grief, and I believe, how to process every difficult situation we face in this life.

Frist, we see His attempt to withdraw to a solitary place. We do not know if He actually got any alone time before the masses caught up to Him, but we get to see His response when they do.

He took compassion them, and then He served them.

Our grief is real. It matters. We do not want to skip or avoid the process. But that does not mean it is all we can do. We are wired to serve. It feels good to help someone else. It is supposed to. You will feel better if you do something for someone else. I promise.

I cannot promise you will actually feel like doing something for someone else. But once you are doing it, or have done it, you will feel better.

Right after my dad died, a couple on our serve team from church had a baby. I did not reach out to them right away; I did not even think about it. And that is ok. But after a couple of weeks, I did think about them, realized they had had their baby, and I had a desire to do something for them. I mentally had the desire, but honestly physically I did not feel like grocery shopping or cooking. I contemplated buying something from a restaurant and I think that would have been fine. But the eighty-year-old woman that lives inside me (She shows up a lot. I call her Pearl.) pushed me to cook something. I made a simple spaghetti casserole and took it to their house. We all chatted for a few minutes and I got to meet their precious new baby girl. It felt amazing. I felt alive.

After Jesus had served the people, oh and don't miss the fact that a massive miracle took place at that time, He circled back around to His previous plan. He went away to a solitary place.

What did He do there? He was not on His phone, and He was not watching TV. He was not on His computer either. He probably couldn't get Wi-Fi in such a remote place. No, none of that. After He made some space to be alone, He prayed. He spent time with the Lord and He gave Himself space and time to process and feel.

Now hear me. I am not saying in a season of grief that we can never watch TV or be on our phones or computer. I'm not. Believe me (and my husband will tell you), I probably watched a full season of *Law and Order* in the weeks after my dad died. Plus, half a season of *Beverly Hills 90210*. Some amazing channel started airing the original series just in time.

I did not camp out or get stuck there. I needed a few minutes of distraction, but I did not completely isolate. I also spent time alone in the presence of God. I sat with my Savior, my Savior who understood my grief and all I was feeling. If we want to remain on the journey to joy in a season of grief, we cannot do it without the Lord. Even if we feel like we have nothing to say, we can still go sit in His presence.

Maybe for five minutes at first. Maybe all we do is sit and cry. That is enough.

It is always a good idea to follow Jesus' example. In grieving we see He pulled away to be alone, but then He felt compassion for others and served them.

We also see Jesus expressing grief through emotion. Specifically, through crying.

"Jesus wept".[88]

It is the shortest verse in the bible but one of the most profound. I am a crier. For sure. I cry. Often. Daily maybe. It is just part of who I am, and I have been that way always. But in the first weeks after dad died, I did not cry. I cried the day I found out. I could not stop crying. But after everyone had been told that my dad had passed, there was a shift into all that had to be done. Being the one who lived closest to dad and had all the information, I became the hub. Honestly, I was glad to be. My mind shifted into "doing" mode. I became the event director for the week, and I think I kind of separated myself from it all emotionally. I still do not know if that was my own doing or protection from God. I do not know that I could have done both at the same time; grieve emotionally and make the decisions we had to make, host the family at our house, greet and console others in pain. I had family coming in that frankly, only I knew. I had a role that needed to be filled, and I was glad to fill it. I wanted everyone at my house. I loved all the conversation and voices from my childhood of uncles and cousins filling my home. I treasure that time. It was a good week in that sense. Dad would have loved it. He loved the chance to be together with family. Looking at photos and swapping old stories. But I felt like if I started crying, really started crying, I would not stop. So somehow, I just didn't. And I think that was ok that first week.

88. John 11:35

After the first week, the tears did come, as they needed to. God created us to feel and to process those feelings. Having emotions through it all is part of how we are supposed to process.

The best part of Jesus' example is how He does it all. He grieves and He process but He does not stop living out His purpose.

We don't have to either. We just learned how important our God-given purpose is. When the difficult seasons come it can be tempting to put everything else on hold. We feel we can't be who God is asking us to be in the midst of our pain. But can I challenge us a bit on that thinking? God challenged me so I am just passing it on to you.

My dad died on March 10. I had agreed months earlier to speak at and emcee an annual women's conference called The Brave Gathering. It is a wonderful event that I look forward to every year. But my dad *just* died. So, now what? Now what turned out to be: I let God use me. Use me to pour out an incredible message, that could only have been from Him, to share His goodness and power with a group of women who wanted an encounter with God.

We walk in our purpose with God because we know what He created us to do. We know who He created us to be. And we can walk that out because we have taken the time to allow Him to give us complete freedom and healing in all the areas we need it.

We are now free to walk in all the joy with Him!

THE JOY JOURNEY

THE JOY JOURNEY

"And everlasting joy will be yours"[89]

You did it! Yay! You made it through. You walked the journey. Connecting or reconnecting to God and discovering all He has for you is cause for celebration. God is a god of celebration, did you know?

I will show you.

Have you read the story of the Prodigal Son in the Bible? I love this story! So much! My editor and publisher has really been teaching me a lot about using exclamation points and using them *very* sparingly. I admit I am an exclamation point over user. I have practiced a miraculous amount of restraint so far, but we are almost done and seriously, this story is amazing, so Jacquetta, I apologize in advance because I am about to overuse the heck out of some exclamation points!

Seriously, this story is so good. You can read all about it in Luke 15:11-32 but if you'll indulge me one last SaraPhrase, I'll paint you a picture.

A son is living with his family on his father's estate and decides he is bored and wants to go live it up in the big city. The problem is he has no money of his own. So, he goes to his dad and basically says, "Hey dad, when you die I know I will get half your stuff. But I really do not want to have to wait so, it's not that I wish you were

---

89. Isaiah 61:7

dead or anything, but can I have my half now so I can go live it up and party hardy?"

The dad agrees to his request and gives him half of his estate and the son heads off for bright lights and the big city. It does not go so well though. Seems the son lacks some maturity and wisdom so he blows the entire inheritance and before too long, junior finds himself broke and desperate and hungry in every sense of the word.

Thankfully, he wises up and decides to go home where he can at least ask to be a servant in his dad's home where he will have food to eat and a roof over his head. While he is still a long way from home, his dad, who must have been keeping an eye out, sees him coming from far in the distance. What does dad do? He drops everything and runs to his son.

> *"But while he was still a long way off, his father saw him and was filled with compassion for him; he ran to his son, threw his arms around him and kissed him."*[90]

Do you notice anything familiar in that verse?

Remember our story of Jesus after John the Baptist was murdered? Jesus is on His way to spend time with the Lord and grieve His loss and what happens? The people come and they want time with Jesus for themselves. What does Jesus do?

> *"When Jesus landed and saw a large crowd, he had compassion on them and healed their sick."*[91]

As Jesus has compassion for the crowd, the father has compassion for his prodigal son. Spoiler alert: both are pictures of our Father's compassion for us.

Y'all. This story is amazing! There is so much that God has for us in this parable. We are all the prodigal son in one sense or another.

90. Luke 15:20
91. Matthew 14:14

We have all gone astray on our own and neglected the One who loves us the most. When we come back, we realize that not only has our Father been keeping a lookout for us so that He sees us coming from far off in the distance, but He is ready, not with a lecture and a scolding but with open and loving arms. He wraps us in an embrace full of healing as He speaks our identity over us and reminds us we are free, we are His and we are home.

Do you know what happens next?

He says it's time to PARTAY!

The son starts in with his rehearsed speech of sorrow and regret, but the Father is having none of it. The Father is not concerned with what happened or why it happened. His son is home, and he wants to celebrate. And celebrate they do. The text says immediately that "they began to celebrate". Drop everything and have some fun! Celebrate with joy!

What a perfect ending to the story. Except it was not quite the ending for them and it is not quite the ending for us either. Just as the party was really getting good, a new character enters the picture. The older brother.

While our scene of reconciliation and jubilation unfolded, the older brother was off working in the fields. He comes home to find the party of the century in full swing and inquires as to what is going on. A servant lets him know his brother is home and dad is throwing an epic bash to celebrate.

Does the brother jump for joy and head in to welcome him home and grab some food? Sadly, no.

Does the brother get misty eyed realizing he thought he might never see his younger brother ever again and now he knows he is home safe and sound? Nope.

The older brother has himself a good, old-fashioned tantrum. He gets mad and refuses to go to the party inside, instead he proceeds to throw himself a big ole' pity party right there on the lawn. What happens next is crucial, more than crucial. Let me check the thesaurus. It is imperative, central, compelling, pivotal and vital that we get this.

When you and I discover more of God and His goodness and more of His joy, we are going to change for the better. As we should. We are becoming healthy and free and we are discovering who God created us to be and what He created us to do! It is exciting! It is time to celebrate!

Unfortunately, there might be some in our lives who like the old us. We fit better into their picture of life the way we were. Our growth, for some reason, might make some uncomfortable. Everyone might not be as happy for us as we wish they were. They might not want to celebrate with us like we wish they would.

It is ok. There will be plenty who are happy and do want to celebrate. Find them. Share with them, celebrate like crazy with them! Find those who will rejoice with you while you rejoice![92]

What about those who do not seem to want to come into the party with us? I am glad you asked. I had that conversation with God over the course of writing this book. He showed me this story of the prodigal son, but He showed me a part I had never noticed before. And what He showed me floored me and changed my life.

In the past, when I sensed someone was not interested in joining me in a party season to celebrate God and His goodness, I would leave my fun little shindig with the Lord and go out to see what I could do to convince them. I took off my party hat to make them feel more comfortable since they didn't feel like celebrating and felt more like sulking.

But that's not what the prodigal son did:

"The older brother became angry and refused to go in. So his father went out and pleaded with him."[93]

The Father went out and pleaded with him. The son stayed put at the party. Y'all, we cannot miss this. It is ok to stay put and enjoy the party, enjoy the life your Father has given you.

---

92. Romans 12:15
93. Luke 15:28

It's not about being heartless or self-centered or compassionless - the older brother was not hurt or in need. He was throwing a fit and refusing to celebrate with his Father. The younger son could not have fixed that. We have to trust these people in our lives to God. We love them and pray for them, but we don't try to go convince them to be happy for us and with us. Let the Father do what only the Father can do.

You put your party hat back on and get to dancing!

THE JOURNEY CONTINUES...

We have walked the *Journey to Joy* with the Lord and seen His truth for our healing, freedom, identity and purpose.

There is an initial time of learning and going through the journey and then I believe we are equipped to repeat the steps of our journey as we continue through life. The first time we find deep healing for things of our past and freedom from strong areas of bondage. We get to walk in that healing and freedom for the rest of our lives. But we also live in a fallen world with imperfect people. You and I are imperfect. There will continue to be things that wound us. There will be new things that we need to forgive ourselves and others for.

Bringing these things to God and forgiving and moving forward is continuous. Daily. Especially if we notice that our joy seems to be hindered, we need to sit with God and ask if there are areas of unhealth we have let go unchecked. Let Him be our great Physician and bring us back to a place of health and wholeness again and again.

The journeying becomes a regular part of our lives.

Remember the grill analogy in the Freedom Journey about my experience with depression?

The same applies here. To keep walking in joy with the Lord, we have to stay healthy and free.

We have to lay down false identities and remind ourselves who we really are in Christ. And we have to walk out and step into all that He has called us to.

We go through the work and get on the right course with God, but as life happens around us and to us, it is easy to veer off course. That is why, from time to time, it is good to check in and see how we are doing. How am I in the area of healing and freedom? Has my identity taken any hits lately? Am I walking out my purpose? How is my joy right now?

The *Journey to Joy Companion Journal* can help greatly with this. But any journal you have will do. Jot these questions down from time to time and honestly answer them. Then take the steps with the Lord to get back where you need to be.

When we do, everlasting joy will be ours.

Do not get frustrated along the way if God leads you on a path that is not completely clear.

Remember how I told you writing this book was so very difficult for me? I am very visual, and the fact that I could not see the path or an outline for this book made it very frustrating for me. It made it hard to know where to begin since I didn't know where I was going. It was so frustrating at times.

Especially in the beginning. I wanted, what I now know is called, a Narrative Sprint Movie Montage. You know what I am talking about even if you didn't know that it had a name. It usually happens in movies where the main character is going through some big transformation or learning something new. Of course, the movie is not going to show the actual time it takes for the character to work on their project each and every day. They edit a bunch of clips together, put it to a song and in 60 seconds, six months has gone by and they have mastered the skill, had the makeover, or trained for the fight. It sprints the narrative forward in time. That is exactly what I wanted. A nice little montage, pictures of me in different outfits on different days sitting down at my computer to write and at the end of the song my book would be complete! Voila!

Unfortunately, I did not get a movie montage. I had to show up every day and do the work, even though I was not always sure in what direction I was headed. Of course, along the way, as I was obedient to meet God at my keyboard and write, the picture began to take shape. It became clearer. I still could not see the book, the outline or the sections. But keywords became prominent - healing, freedom, identity, purpose. Those four words. They became my road maps, my marker stones.

And then one miraculous weekend when I got away by myself to write, God did one of those unbelievable things that only He can do.

As I wrote and studied, God led me to Isaiah 61. It made sense because Isaiah 61 is the passage I was doing a study on in my apartment in my late twenties when God first gave me a vision for a future ministry. It was a Bible study by Beth Moore called *Breaking Free* and in it she spent time on Isaiah 61. Parts of it were etched onto my heart and it was a passage of Scripture I loved.

It was familiar and brought a smile to my face to have the Lord lead me back there. He reminded me about the vision He had given me so many years before. But He wasn't just taking me back to reminisce. No, He took me back in order to launch me forward.

As I read through Isaiah 61, He began to take the four words I had been hearing, healing, freedom, identity and purpose, and show me their place in the passage.

It looked something like this:

> The Spirit of the Sovereign Lord is on me,
>> because the Lord has anointed me
>> to proclaim good news to the poor.
> He has sent me to bind up the brokenhearted, - HEALING
>> to proclaim freedom for the captives - FREEDOM
>> and release from darkness for the prisoners, - FREEDOM
>
> to proclaim the year of the Lord's favor
>> and the day of vengeance of our God,
> to comfort all who mourn, - HEALING
>
>> and provide for those who grieve in Zion--
> to bestow on them a crown of beauty

    instead of ashes, - HEALING
the oil of joy
    instead of mourning, - HEALING
and a garment of praise
    instead of a spirit of despair. - HEALING
They will be called oaks of righteousness,
    a planting of the Lord
      for the display of his splendor. - IDENTITY

They will rebuild the ancient ruins - PURPOSE
    and restore the places long devastated;
they will renew the ruined cities
    that have been devastated for generations. - PURPOSE

Strangers will shepherd your flocks;
    foreigners will work your fields and vineyards.

And you will be called priests of the Lord,
    you will be named ministers of our God. - IDENTITY
You will feed on the wealth of nations,
    and in their riches you will boast.

Instead of your shame
    you will receive a double portion, - HEALING,
      FREEDOM, IDENTITY AND PURPOSE
and instead of disgrace
    you will rejoice in your inheritance. PURPOSE
And so you will inherit a double portion in your land,
    PURPOSE

It was so exciting! The words I thought were so random and could not figure out how they fit into a book, were laid out perfectly on the page.

But where was joy? Is the main idea of this book not joy anymore Lord? As I posed the question to Him, He urged me to read on. I got to the last line of this passage - after God's people had experienced healing and freedom and received His identity and purpose for their lives - and I read:

"and everlasting joy will be yours."

Y'all, I about fell out of my chair:

They will experience healing, freedom, identity and purpose, and then everlasting joy will be theirs. There was my book!

The path there was not clear for a long time. At least not to me. It was confusing and frustrating, and I struggled. I recently came across a desperate prayer I wrote out among some original notes and ideas about the book:

"Lord, I do not know how to write this book. I do not know what this book is. I have no idea what to do or how to do it. I am very frustrated. What am I doing? I feel this deep, overwhelming calling, but what am I supposed to do? One minute I think I am heading in the right direction and the next day I feel so lost and unsure of everything."

Thankfully, I stayed the course. God was guiding, so I knew it was wise to follow. It was a journey I never could have taken on my own. I am so grateful it was part of my story to take it with Him and share it with you.

He always has a journey for us to take with Him, and it is always in our best interest to take it.

Take a step. Keep taking steps. Keep walking with Him.

Continue to receive His healing and freedom. Walk in your true identity and fulfill your God- given purpose, and everlasting JOY will be yours.

The Spirit of the Sovereign Lord is on me,
    because the Lord has anointed me
    to proclaim good news to the poor.
He has sent me to bind up the brokenhearted,
    to proclaim freedom for the captives
    and release from darkness for the
prisoners,

to proclaim the year of the Lord's favor
    and the day of vengeance of our God,
to comfort all who mourn,
    and provide for those who grieve in Zion—
to bestow on them a crown of beauty
    instead of ashes,
the oil of joy
    instead of mourning,
and a garment of praise
    instead of a spirit of despair.
They will be called oaks of righteousness,
    a planting of the Lord
    for the display of his splendor.

They will rebuild the ancient ruins
    and restore the places long devastated;
they will renew the ruined cities
    that have been devastated for
generations.
Strangers will shepherd your flocks;
    foreigners will work your fields and
vineyards.
And you will be called priests of the Lord,
    you will be named ministers of our God.
You will feed on the wealth of nations,
    and in their riches you will boast.

Instead of your shame
    you will receive a double portion,
and instead of disgrace
    you will rejoice in your inheritance.
And so you will inherit a double portion in
your land,
    and everlasting joy will be yours.

Isaiah 61:1-7

YOUR JOY JOURNEY

Let's Get Practical

Joy is a fruit of the Spirit. It is a gift from God. Ultimately it comes from Him. Sometimes we feel it with our whole selves, other times it is a belief and a promise we hold on to. The feelings will come and go. But the real joy we always have access to. We can experience it always.

I do believe there are things we can do to feel more joy. Simple things. Smile. Pay someone a compliment. Serve someone. Put someone before you in any way you can. Listen to your favorite upbeat song. Worship! Praise God! Dance! Moving even when you don't feel like it isn't faking it. You aren't pretending. You are doing it based on what you believe, not on what you feel. Find a way to laugh. There are so many funny animal videos online. You could be laughing for days. Be proactive. Be willing to be aggressive. Take matters into your own hands. If you want your mood to change, then change your mood. I believe most of the time we can. I am talking about being grumpy or in a bad mood or feeling a little down. I'm not talking about clinical depression, although I do believe these things help there too.

One of the practical things I developed during this journey is The Joy Scale. It is by no means scientific, but it does work. It is a simple tool that helps us identify the things that increase or decrease our joy. None of these things are the source for our joy. We have gotten that through our relationship with God and walking in healing, freedom, identity and purpose. And now, and always, we can experience joy because of Him.

We are spiritual. We are also practical. God created us with the ability to laugh and have fun and enjoy life! When we can find those things that bring joy and add them to our life, we are simply maximizing what He has given us.

I wholeheartedly believe Jesus was a fun guy. I think He enjoyed the people He did life with. He lived out His purpose first and foremost, but I believe He enjoyed it along the way. I do not think the people would have followed the way they did, invited Him to weddings and dinners and parties the way they did, if Jesus was not fun to be around. You do not invite unfun people to those things, even if they can turn your water into wine.

So, let's find out what brings the fun and what kills it. Once we are aware, we are able to adjust accordingly whenever and wherever we can.

THE JOY SCALE

Choosing joy means choosing to be joyful. Choosing to smile sometimes even when we do not feel like it and then realizing we feel better after. It means choosing joy. But it also, and maybe even more so, means choosing the things that we know bring us joy. And maybe even not choosing things that we know rob our joy. Sound familiar? We already got to practice this when we started our journey. We brought the Joy Cultivators with us and left the Joy Killers, that weighed down our luggage, behind.

I created a Joy Scale to help show you what I mean.

Here's how the joy scale works-

We measure using a scale of 1-10:

    1 - it completely zaps or steals our joy
    5 - somewhat neutral
    10 - bring us lots of joy!

Something is a 10 for sure if when you think of it or write it down you smile big on the inside and the outside.

One thing that brings joy is being present and more aware in our own lives. The Joy Scale will help us do that. I cannot control 100% of what is in my life and what I have to do in my life. Much like in the area of giftedness, I cannot do what I feel I was created to do 100% of the time. I will not be able to just do things that are at the

222

top of my joy scale 100% of the time. However, I do have significant influence.

The Joy Scale can help us identify little or big things that maybe we did not realize drain our joy or build it up. The week I first used the scale, my husband and I were watching a silly TV show called *The Masked Singer*. Maybe you know it or watch it too. We ended up loving it. Each week I really looked forward to us watching it together. When I put it on my Joy Scale, it was a 10! I realized how much we laughed while we watched. We both enjoyed using our detective skills, trying to figure out who each masked singer really is and then seeing the reveal each time. The Joy Scale helped me recognize how much I enjoyed watching the show together, so this activity became a higher priority for me.

Let's stick with TV programs for a minute. I am a firm believer that too much TV is never a good thing. Binge watching and numbing out our minds does not do us much good. I have experienced that personally. Sometimes what I think I need is a day of nothing and just mind numbing with a show or movies, but I do not actually feel any better at the end of the day and oftentimes I even feel worse.

Additionally, in my experience, even a small amount of the wrong show can have an impact on my joy. I used to watch a show called *Criminal Minds*. I love pretty much all cop crime drama shows. *Criminal Minds* though was a bit different for me. It was darker. More gruesome. I even experienced some fear in that season as a result of that show. I was single and living alone and all of a sudden had some bad dreams and then fear in my home for no reason I could come up with other than I had taken up watching that show. I stopped. And the fear disappeared: That show would rank very low on my Joy Scale. Basically, a zero.

It is good to think about why something ranks where it does on your scale. If I had thought watching *The Masked Singer* was just about watching TV, I would have probably placed it lower on the scale and I would have been wrong. A big part, probably the main part, of why watching *The Masked Singer* was so fun for me was that my hubby and I did it together. We have lots of fun and interaction watching that show. We are also excellent judges of singing even though neither of us can carry a tune.

My encouragement to you is to first evaluate how much TV you are watching and then look at what you watch and whether those things bring joy or steal it.

Other things on my Joy Scale:

Chores around the house. I found that the act of doing those chores did not necessarily bring me much joy, so they did not rank very high. But *completing* those same tasks did bring joy, it was a seven or eight at times. Therefore, in order to get to the joy of having them complete, I had to do them.

Walking my dog was an interesting one. Most of the time it was high on my joy scale. I like being outside. Many times, I listened to worship music while we walked, and all of that brings me great joy. But there are days where it is too hot or too cold to be excited about going. But being healthy is an important priority for me and feeling good ranks high on the joy scale, so it works as a motivator to help me get out the door and get going.

Going to the movies (the right kinds of movies for me) is high on my joy scale. It is a family tradition to go to premier nights on Thursdays when movies we like come out. I love it. We take up a whole row and it is such a fun thing. We go to a nice dine-in theater and really make an experience out of it. For all of those reasons, it is high on my scale. And I have learned the actual movie does not always matter. As I mentioned before, we took a family outing to the movies the day my dad died.

My dad died early in the morning on a Sunday. From 7:30am till about 10am I was up at the assisted living home where he lived taking care of all of those details that you take care of right away. My husband and mother-in-law were eventually up there with me. Once everything there was done, my husband wrapped his arms around me and said let's go home. I kind of panicked. "Go home and DO

The Joy Journey

WHAT!?" was my thought. My brother was driving up the next day and we would meet with the funeral home. It was still early in the day and I could not imagine what to do with myself for the rest of the day. I looked at my mother-in-law and said, "I think I want to go to the movies." She smiled and said, "we definitely should".

My dad loved the movies. And while he was physically able, he joined us on our big movie outings. So, that afternoon we all headed to the theater. The only thing showing with enough seats for all of us together (my brother-in-law drove over and joined us too) was *The Lego Movie 2*. Nothing against *The Lego Movie 2* but I had never seen the first *Lego Movie*. But it was not about the movie. It was just a way for all of us to be together, do something together on that day. And it was great. I did cry, but it was good. And the movie is actually great. It was a great afternoon that brought me some joy on the hardest day of my life.

It is not possible to eliminate everything that falls below a 5 on our joy scales. But there are some things I can eliminate or have less of. In case I haven't mentioned it yet, complaining and negative conversations steal joy. It does not mean I never catch myself complaining or being super negative, but the point is I catch myself. Then I can change course and try to find the positive.

Drinking alcohol. Oh, gosh, the Christian is going to talk about how drinking is bad. No. I do not think drinking is bad. I think abusing alcohol, drugs, food, entertainment, or anything else is all bad. The "thing" is not always negative on its own, but our use of it certainly can be. But the fact is alcohol is a depressant. Remember my story at the movie theater after my dad died? The truth is, if I have a glass of wine with dinner a few nights in a row, I recognize my mood dips for a few days after. It's something that is true for me and that I am aware of, so it affects where it lands on my scale.

Part of the journey is also discovering new things that bring joy that maybe you do not even realize are there. I highly encourage you to be adventurous. Try new things. The companion Joy Journal is a great tool to help you do this. Evaluate your joy adventures with your joy scale and see how they do. Go to a museum. Take a hike. (not get out of here, but actually go outside and walk around). Ride a bike.

Walk a dog. Go to the theater. Smile at a stranger. Do a random act of kindness, or a not so random one. Find an old record shop, a thrift store. Figure out a day trip, take a drive. Go to the zoo! You are also free to give any or all of those things a 1 on your scale. My friend tried macrame recently and when she was done, promptly threw it across the room and swore never to do it again. So, that's a 1 for her. But now she knows!

Social Media. After taking a year off of Facebook, I came back to find that I could more easily filter my feed to where I pretty much just see videos of babies and animals and of course, baby animals. It's great! When I left Facebook, it was most definitely stealing my joy and I was letting it. When I felt it was time to come back, I was determined to make sure I didn't make the same mistakes. I filtered out all I did not want to see. I choose not to get my "news" through Facebook. There are news sites I can go to for that. On Facebook I really just want to see updates from friends, family and old acquaintances, and things that make me smile or laugh. A few good recipe ideas are also great to see. And then there are all these baby animal videos. So great! So much joy! I love Facebook now.

Avoid the "must be nice" trap. Recognize when you are in it and get out! You see someone you know that bought a new house, went on a great trip, got flowers for "no reason" and you think to yourself "Must be nice. I wish I could afford to take a vacation like that." Stop! Abandon ship! Close the browser, close the app, run, do not walk, away! You are falling into the trap of comparison and the enemy just stole your joy. Unless you sincerely mean, "Oh, that is so nice for her. She really deserves it and I am happy for her." But if that is not the case, catch yourself immediately, look up and list a few things you are grateful for.

Spend some time on social media. Afterwards rate how you feel on your joy scale. If it is not a 6 or higher, I recommend making some changes. Maybe you need to take a break. Look at filtering out negative stories, headlines, or people. I am a firm believer in unfollowing those who are consistently negative or divisive in what they post. For me, that sucks my joy. For you, if it does not somehow then by all means keep scrolling. But the simple fact is enough negative in is going to have an impact on how we feel:

"A good man brings good things out of the good stored up in his heart, and an evil man brings evil things out of the evil stored up in his heart. For the mouth speaks what the heart is full of."[94]

"Above all else, guard your heart, for everything you do flows from it."[95]

"You brood of vipers, how can you who are evil say anything good? For the mouth speaks what the heart is full of."[96]

"Those who live according to the flesh have their minds set on what the flesh desires; but those who live in accordance with the Spirit have their minds set on what the Spirit desires. The mind governed by the flesh is death, but the mind governed by the Spirit is life and peace."[97]

Therefore, as God's chosen people, holy and dearly loved, clothe yourselves with compassion, kindness, humility, gentleness and patience. Bear with each other and forgive one another if any of you has a grievance against someone. Forgive as the Lord forgave you. And over all these virtues put on love, which binds them all together in perfect unity.

"Let the peace of Christ rule in your hearts, since as members of one body you were called to peace. And be thankful."[98]

See, told you.

---

94. Luke 6:45
95. Proverbs 4:23
96. Matthew 12:34
97. Romans 8:5-6
98. Colossians 3:12-15

All that is left to do is start making your list of activities. Spend a week or so just jotting down the things you do regularly. Maybe make a note about how you feel while you do the activity or how you feel when it's done.

When you have some time, create your joy scale and start placing your items. You can also just assign a number 1-10 to a list of things if you prefer.

I recommend having some sort of journal where you can keep track. Note the things you can limit or remove. Or is there a different way to look at them like me with my chores and walking the dog? The Journey to Joy Companion Journal has ample space for you to keep track.

Whatever approach you take, the goal is to be aware of the things in your life that bring you joy and that take it away and then to make adjustments where you can.

Before we part, I cannot miss one final opportunity to remind you about the point of this all:

"in Your presence, there is fullness of joy;"[99]

The most important thing to remember is that all joy comes from and is available because of God. We will never experience true, lasting joy apart from Him. He created us to feel joy and because of Him we can. Never separate Him from your pursuit of joy. Pursue God, be on a journey with God and you will be on a Journey to Joy. The world has nothing for us, all we seek is found in Him, including joy!

Happy journeying!

---

99. Psalm 16:11 ESV

JOY SCALE

Activity	Ranking 1 - 10

The People to Thank Page
(uh, a Chapter at this point)

Do you remember when Julia Roberts won an Oscar for her role in *Erin Brockovich*? Probably not, but for some reason I do. They were trying to keep the speeches short that year, but she warned everyone she was not even going to attempt to be brief. She said, "I may never be here again." And then she proceeded to thank all who had helped her get to that point in her career. At one point she said, "Thank you to…everyone I've ever met in my life." She closed her speech by saying, "I love the world! I'm so happy! Thank you!"

I can relate to all of Mrs. Roberts' sentiments.

That's why I am about to attempt to thank "everyone I've ever met in my life." Because something about the process of writing and publishing a book inspires you to look back and reflect and be in awe. So many incredible people have inspired me, encouraged me and poured into my life in some way. This is my attempt to actually thank them all. And by all I mean all. It has become its own special project here at the end because my life would not look much like it does if not for so many amazing people.

But you're under no obligation to read it all. Unless you are like me and feel compelled to read every word on every page. In that case, I'm a little sorry. But as you read hopefully it will inspire gratitude in your heart for all the people who have helped you become today's version of you and helped you get to places you always wanted to be. You don't have to write a book to formally thank them. Grab a note and send them a heartfelt thank you of your own.

My Lord, my God, my Father in Heaven, thank you.

This was hard. I know I told you I didn't want to do it a few different times. I think I may have even told you I wasn't going to do it. Sorry about that. Thank you for not believing me but instead believing in me. I know you've heard this before but, you were right. I'm so incredibly glad and honored you asked me to do this. It was so fun to do it with you and see you work miracle after miracle. You are amazing and I love you. Thank you for giving me every word to write. I never, ever in a hundred thousand million years could have done this without you. And I think we both know that's no exaggeration. You are my everything and I can do nothing without you. Thank you for being faithful even when I was not. Thank you for finding me, picking me up, cleaning me off and giving me the gift of your Son, Jesus. Thank you for your unending love. A love that secured my future, redeemed my past, and brought joy into my present.

My life is full beyond anything I could have hoped or imagined. I'm so grateful to be on this journey with you, and I can't wait to see where we go next!

Paul, I don't know how many times I've read this statement in a book (yes, I read ALL the pages in every book, including the "Who to Thank" page) but <u>NONE of this would have been possible without you</u>. Your selfless sacrifices, hard work and dedication for our family. Your patience with all the seasons we have walked through that impacted our home, our lives and sometimes your dinner. ;) You've always called out these gifts in me and encouraged me and when God said "Go" you were right there ready for the ride. The hours and hours you spent reading Journey to Joy and providing valuable insight and ideas has helped make this book what it is. Thank you. You were so worth the wait and I love you, our life, our family and our story. You are the best part of my joy journey. (no I'm not crying as I type this… oh whatever, yes, of course I am crying as I type this!) I love you so much and I like you so much and I'm so looking forward to the rest of the journey with you.

Caleb, Riley, Remi - Being your stepmom is my greatest blessing, just after the blessing of being married to your dad. What a joy to have each of you in my life!

Caleb - You are a man after God's heart. He has created you uniquely with so many interests and talents. I love that He gave us so many in common: books, movies, good food and of course, Jesus. How you pursue God and His calling for your life inspires me. You are a leader, a teacher and a pastor, regardless of the profession you choose. God has gifted you in many ways, and I am so proud of the man you are becoming. You have always been full of life and fun and having you as the son God had for me brings me joy! I love you!

Riley - You are a beloved daughter. To God and to me and in every way possible. The Lord has given you so much passion and steadfastness. Your dedication to your pursuits inspires me. You are hardworking, loyal, thoughtful and caring. And you make great parking signs. (Yes, I still have it. ;) God placed that empathy and love in you on purpose, and He will guide you to do great things. You are growing into the most interesting, beautiful and wise young woman. The best is yet to be, and I am so excited to see it all unfold! I love you!

Remi - Literally from the day we met your smile has meant the world to me. You know I don't throw that word around casually. It was literally that first moment we met. That little girl looking up and smiling at me made me feel like I could do this stepmom thing. :) You are a leader, an encourager and a beloved daughter to God and to me. The way you walk through life and overcome obstacles and difficulties inspires me. You carry joy and light and laughter in you always. Keep sharing it. The Lord has great plans for you. I love you! — Stepmother. ;)

Dad. I don't know how heaven works, so I don't know if there's even a way for you to know this stuff. Thankfully, we left nothing unsaid while you were here, and I have no regrets. I'm grateful we had the time for all of that. I guess I just want to acknowledge, somewhere, how much joy it brought me to be your daughter. How grateful I am that I got to be the one with you to care for you in those last years. I wouldn't have traded that role for anything. I'm so grateful for all the amazing times we had together. You taught me to go with the flow. Not to get upset about much. To have fun, especially on vacation. And I cherish every memory of those times. Especially flying through the air on zip lines in the rainforest in Alaska! How many girls get to say they did that with their dad? I miss you every day. Thank you for knowing Jesus, for loving Jesus, and for telling me about Jesus.

A special thank you to my Uncle Kermit and my cousin Susan for helping me fill in the gaps of our handed down family stories and my sometimes-vague little girl memories. I love you!

Mom, thank you for being a writer and sharing your stories with me and thank you for all the editing tips. They have been put to good use! Thank you for always encouraging me to write and to write honestly without filters. Journey to Joy is a better book because of the things you taught me. I love you.

Clint - Thank you for being the best big brother a girl could ask for. You loved me, you played with me, you taught me all about sports, you protected me, you defended me and then one time you convinced me our TV was going to blow up just so you could mess with me for a day - so, not a flawless record but still, pretty exceptional. Thank you for going first and then holding my hand when it came time to walk through the tough parts of life. I can't imagine having to navigate dad's journey without you. Thank you for always being there and always knowing what to say. And thanks for wanting to pour water on the girls who were mean to me. I love you!

Vickie - How did I make it 35 years without you? You radiate the joy of the Lord to me and to our entire family. The blessings you are passing down from generation to generation are priceless. Thank you for loving me unconditionally and being my biggest fan. I love you. Now, let's go eat some sushi and spend some gift cards!

Joel, Simone, Jax, Jim, Gayle, Ralph, Anita & Shardá - You are each proof that my journey is only getting better and better and better. I love you and I'm so thankful for you!

Peggy, Jason, Emily & Jagger - Family is precious and I'm so gratefull y'all are mine! Y'all have always brought me joy and you have been family when I needed it the most. I love you!

Gary - I would not have known what kind of stepparent I wanted to be without you. Thank you for loving me like I was your own and loving me well. I love you.

It Takes a Village to Write a Book

Amy, Crys, Jami, Kara, Laurie - AKA: My Little Ponies - Yes, I put it in here. That's what's so great about our 40s. We care less about being weird and no one else understanding. How is it possible we've done nearly 2 decades of life together? Because we met when we were 2, right? You are each my fellow joy journey-ers and supporters. You've walked with me through it all, you've seen it all and stayed, anyway. You and your prayers held me up so many times throughout this journey. You love me well. Plus, you had amazing ideas for Journey to Joy that became actual realities that people will experience because of you. (I'm enjoying a Cup of Joy right now!) Thank you, I love you! Here's to 20 more!

Barbie - I love God's perfect timing! The way He brought us and our stories together was divine. Thank you for believing in me and trusting me with a microphone. Talk about being Brave! :) Thank you for sharing all your writing and publishing wisdom with me!

I am so glad God decided we would get to journey together in this season. Thanks for being my phone friend!

Cynthia - Thank you for being such a cheerleader and believer in Journey to Joy! Thank you for following your dreams and inspiring me and others to do the same. Making new friends is tough. In your late 30's it's even tougher. Thanks for saying yes and wanting to be my frien!

Julie - My friend. At the end of this marathon, you were there taking my calls, telling me I could do it, speaking truth and giving me God's wisdom and living water to help me finish. Thank you for being my coach! You encourage and speak truth and celebrate when I want to celebrate and push when I need to be pushed and let me whine a little when I want to whine, but just until it's time to tell me to get up and keep going. I don't know if I would have crossed the finish line without you. Thank you. I love you, our story and our friendship!

Karen - The best kind of Karen! Thanks for all the Sonic runs and long conversations over avocado toast. Thank you for encouraging me and checking on me and praying for me and inviting me on girl's trips! You give Karens a good name! Now let's finish *your* book!

All the joy journey-ers who have shared their stories and prayed for me during this process - I could not have done this without each of you joining the journey along the way. You believed in me. Coached me. Encouraged me. Pushed me. You helped me get to the finish line and for that I am forever grateful! You bring joy to my life.

Chris, that includes you. And thank you for the divine and inspired introduction to…

Jacquetta - You are the best blessing and surprise I didn't know was waiting for me at the finish line! If I'd known, I would have gotten here sooner! Thank you for your wisdom and experience and counsel. All your ideas have been gold and you've made Journey to Joy so much more than it would have been without you! I know this is just the beginning for us and I can't wait to see all that God has in store! (I placed all the exclamation points and contractions you wouldn't let me use in the book, in your "thank you". You're welcome!)

Shveta – I am so thankful for you and our friendship. God is so cool how He crossed our paths and continues to knit our hearts together. I enjoy all of our tea dates and learning about you and your family and your life. Thank you for your friendship and kindness and constant enthusiasm and support for Journey to Joy. God uses you to bring me joy!

My pastor, John Stickl, I did not know all that God had in store for me when He brought me to Valley Creek. A husband, a family, but so much more. Much of your wisdom is sprinkled throughout these pages. Being under your teaching for the last 7 years has definitely left its mark, and it's made me better. Thank you for leading the way you do, teaching the way you do, and caring the way you do. Thank you for the wisdom and counsel and support throughout this process!

Pastors Ed and Lisa Young, I never would have experienced ministry the way I did if not for both of you and all you do in your journeys with God. Your fingerprints are on me and my story and all I do. The foundation I received during my decade with you is priceless to me. I didn't know I was a teacher; I didn't know I was called to ministry, until you gave me the opportunity to grow and discover who God created me to be. I am forever grateful. Thank you.

Donnie - Thank you for always asking me how the book was going. Many times, I didn't want you to ask because I felt like it was not going well, or I was ready for it not to be going at all. But in your own way you held me accountable to what I said I wanted to do and

236

what I believed God had asked me to do. So, thank you! You and Robin are a blessing to me.

Andy - Thank you for telling me to just write my story. Yes, it annoyed me at the time. But God used you because the message was from Him and it was exactly what I needed to hear. Thank you!

Terri Carver, Cecilia Bacon and Debra DeMoss – Wow. Power team. I learned about godly homes, marriages and families from each of you. Thank you for being willing to open up your lives and share your wisdom and your love with me. You made me better.

Janay - I am so grateful that my journey has included you! A wonderful season of my life is filled with amazing memories of doing life and ministry with you. I learned so much by your example and your friendship has always brought me joy!

Denise - When I think of our friendship I immediately hear your laughter in my ears and it makes me smile. I love seeing the miracles God is doing through this journey and I know He has one for you. Enjoy the journey, it is very much for you. And enjoy your bookmark! It is definitely for you!

Tammy! - Thank you! Thank you for listening to God and playing matchmaker for Him. Thank you for your wisdom and guidance and counsel and the occasional kick in the pants that I needed. I am so thankful for you!

Becca – Thank you for taking the time to show me how to heal and how to rest and how to enjoy a new season with God. Thank you for loving me through my grief and letting me talk about my daddy. And thank you for all my "joy" gifts! You have a been a cheerleader and encourager and friend. Thank you.

Don and Suzanne Manning – Thank you for all your support and encouragement. Thank you for believing in *Journey to Joy*, taking the time to recommend it, and share it with your Crazy Cool people.

Mama G – How could I ever forget your smiling face and warm welcome? You were the first and all the rest came because you decided to invest in me. Thank you!

Tony and Emily – Wow. I was at a fork in the road and you were willing to be there for me no matter what. Your prayers got me back on track and because of that, Journey to Joy became a reality. Thank you for your friendship and support and Tony, thanks for being a great boss.

Mark Morgan – Speaking of great bosses. So many wonderful things have happened in my life because of you. You took a young, in every sense of the word, insecure and uncertain employee and coached and led her into something more. You and Jenni accepted me like family and helped me mature and grow in ways I would not have done on my own. Thank you!

To all the VCLA Alum – aka world changers! You inspire me. Thank you for letting me be a tiny part of your journey. Keep pursuing God the way you are. I cannot wait to see your impact on the Kingdom!

Mrs. Beth Moore – We've never met – I did see you one time at a mall in Grapevine, Texas but the God's honest truth is I looked terrible. I was in workout clothes, no make-up and hair amess and I was too embarrassed to accost you, I mean approach you, looking like that. I knew if I tried to articulate what your Bible studies meant to me, I would break down in tears and I wanted to be all dolled up before doing that. I guess I thought a sobbing person with make up on would be less scary than one without. I can't defend my logic but it's why I did not speak to you that day. But what I would have said was, Thank you. Thank you for being willing to step into your calling the way that you have. I know it has not been an easy road. You paved the way for so many and you did it with grace and style and perfect hair. Your studies taught me how to study the Bible and, more importantly, how to fall madly in love with Jesus and scripture. It was through one of your studies that God first called me into ministry and gave me an inkling of all He had in store. He used you in the best way possible in my journey. Thank you.

Mr. Max Lucado – We have never met either and while you don't know me at all, you have been a part of my life since I was a girl. My dad loved your books. He is the one who taught me about Jesus and so he shared all your books with me. *On the Anvil, No Wonder They Call Him Savior, Six Hours One Friday, He Still Moves Stones* and on and on to my most recent, *You Are Never Alone*. I received them as gifts and many times for no reason at all. My dad and I would discuss the stories and I began to get a picture of God and His Son through your eyes. Your words made me laugh and cry and profoundly inspired me in my journey. Thank you for making it fun and intriguing to learn about Jesus and thank you for all the memories you gave me with my dad.

And to anyone I forgot amidst the stupor and brain fog that is this 11th hour – When I awake with a fright at 1am and see your face I'll be sure to send you a note with some free stuff to make up for my oversight. Plus, you'll get a bigger reward than these other folks once you get to heaven. So really, you're welcome.

RESOURCES FOR YOUR JOURNEY

Your Healing Journey

Shame Off You, Alan D. Wright

http://anthemofhope.org

Suicide Crisis Line: 1-800-273-8255

http://www.christiancounselingcenters.org

Your Freedom Journey

Breaking Free, Beth Moore

Your Identity Journey

Follow the Cloud, John Stickl

Your Purpose Journey

Find and Fulfill Purpose, Jacquetta Dantzler

The Gift of Giftedness, Tracy Goyne

Your Joy Journey

How Happiness Happens, Max Lucado

Journey to Joy Companion Journal

Sara
Chapple

Author, Speaker, Coach

For booking inquiries:
sarachapple.com
@heysarachapple

ABOUT THE AUTHOR

Sara Chapple is an author and speaker who has worked in full time ministry for nearly 20 years. She is married to the love of her life, Paul, and their blended bunch consists of 3 amazing teenagers, Caleb, Riley, and Remi, and one fluffy Bichon, London. Sara and her family live in the Dallas, Texas area where they are actively involved in their church. Sara loves working with other communicators as a writing and speaking coach. When she's not working you can find Sara curled up with a cup of hot tea and a good book.

For more information and booking requests please visit www.SaraChapple.com

You can connect with Sara online as @heysarachapple in all the social places.

When I cry out to the LORD, he hears me
and wait patiently for h

" When I cry out to the LORD in times of great joy
and sorrow, he will always answer me. It
might not be ~~an~~ according to my timeline;
but in his perfect timing. ~~I wait for him~~
~~and~~ He will never fails to answer, I simply have
to wait. "

Made in the USA
Columbia, SC
09 October 2021